LITERARY PARIS:
A GUIDE

LITERARY
PARIS:
A GUIDE

JESSICA POWELL

THE LITTLE BOOKROOM

Book design by Katy Homans

Printed in China by South China Printing Co.

title page:
Colette and Missy.
Collection Jouvenel/Centre d'études Colette.

Library of Congress Cataloging-in-Publication Data

Powell, Jessica.
  Literary Paris : a guide / Jessica Powell.
    p. cm.
  ISBN 1-892145-38-3 (hardcover : alk. paper)
  1. Authors, French—Homes and haunts—France—
Paris. 2. Literary landmarks—France—Paris. 3.
Paris (France)—In literature. 4. Paris (France)—
Intellectual life. I. Title.
PQ148.E76 2006
809'.8944361—dc22

                    2006002342

Published by
The Little Bookroom
1755 Broadway, Fifth floor
New York, NY 10019
(212) 293-1643
(212) 333-5374 fax
editorial@littlebookroom.com
www.littlebookroom.com

Contents

Introduction

They followed the embankment, under the plane-trees, seeing the past rise up at every step as the landscape opened out before them: the bridges, their arches cutting across the satin sheen of the river; the Cité covered with shadow, dominated by the yellowing towers of Notre-Dame; the great sweeping curve of the right bank, bathed in sunshine, leading to the dim silhouette of the Pavillion de Flore; the broad avenues, the buildings on either bank, and between them, the Seine, with all the lively activity of its laundry-boats, its baths, its barges.

—Émile Zola
The Masterpiece, 1886

Over the centuries, Paris has been captured on the page so many times that the literary, mythic city is just as real to us as the place itself. The city's rich artistic culture and turbulent history have long captivated the imagination of writers, and few who have lived in Paris have remained neutral about it. Certainly, there are many who have sung its praises. Victor Hugo wrote of its "hot-blooded devotion and tempestuous gaiety," while for Honoré de Balzac it was "the intellectual capital of the world, the stage of your success."

Even writers who were critical of Paris and its culture were unable to resist the city's pull. Molière mocked Parisian high society while struggling to find acceptance in it; Voltaire spent much of his life alternately courting and infuriating the aristocracy. In the nineteenth century, Émile Zola decried the state of the city's poor and the poet Charles Baudelaire lamented the city's rapid modernization—neither, however, could stand to stay away for long. In the twentieth century, the expatriate American Richard Wright tried to leave Paris but realized he no longer belonged anywhere else.

Similarly, the writers who preferred country life seemed unable to completely resist the temptations of the city. Although she set most of her novels outside the French capital, only Paris seemed to offer a woman writer such as George Sand the independence she craved. And Gustave Flaubert—who has gained a reputation as a hermit—nevertheless spent his youth in Paris and drew on his experiences there while writing one of his most famous novels, *Sentimental Education*.

Paris was not an easy city in which to prosper. Molière was forced to hone his skills as a playwright in the provinces after failing in the capital, while the Marquis de Sade found that Paris treated him more kindly when it had him behind bars. And Paul Verlaine and Oscar Wilde both discovered that Paris would toast you one day, then revile you the next.

For centuries, Paris had been the heart of the country's intellectual, political, and artistic life. But as the nineteenth century drew to a close, Paris also became the world capital of modernity, and foreign artists and writers were attracted to its great artistic and social freedom. For Oscar Wilde, Paris was the chance to escape England's Victorian mores; for F. Scott Fitzgerald, it was a respite from New York society life; for James

Baldwin, a refuge from prejudice; for Ernest Hemingway and Mark Twain, an adventure in a new land.

In the early twentieth century, Paris's vibrant cultural scene was producing the most influential art and philosophy of the time. Picasso and the Cubists, Stravinsky and Chagall, the Surrealists and the existentialists all called Paris home. As the American writer Gertrude Stein wrote, "Paris was where the twentieth century was."

Literary Paris explores these writers' lives in the city as well as the Paris portrayed in their works. Wandering about the seventh and eight arrondissements, one still catches sight of the impressive homes of the society women whose salons Marcel Proust frequented—and who became the characters in his masterpiece, *In Search of Lost Time*. Many of the cafés where Ernest Hemingway and Henry Miller wrote still stand, as does the building on the Île St.-Louis where Baudelaire met with the Club des Haschichins to smoke hashish and experience the *paradis artificiels* he would write about in *Les Fleurs du Mal*. One can still have a drink at the cafés and clubs where Jean-Paul Sartre and Simone de Beauvoir ushered in a generation of existentialists or enjoy

a meal at Le Procope, once frequented by Voltaire and later Victor Hugo and the Romantics and the poet Paul Verlaine. And Père Lachaise, where Balzac's character Rastignac challenged Paris, is now the resting place of some of France's most famous writers, statesmen, and artists.

Many of the sites tell stories as dramatic as those in the authors' works: the various apartments where Balzac hid from creditors and the jealous husbands of his mistresses; the Bastille, where the Marquis de Sade provoked protestors just days before the French Revolution; and the theater, where Georges Simenon first courted Josephine Baker.

With its "time-worn stones . . . and the ever-flowing stream beneath the bridges" Zola wrote, Paris is a palpable mix of the past and the present. In Paris, when one goes looking for the past one quickly comes to the same conclusion as Balzac: "While searching the dead I see only the living."

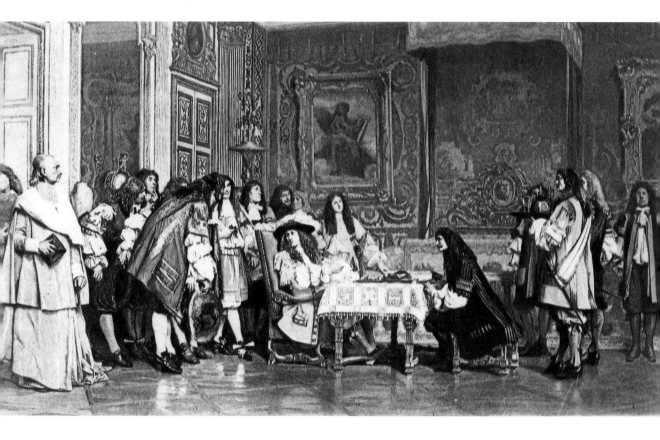

Molière

(1622–1673)

Magdelon: *One must be the antipodes of reason not to confess that Paris is the great bureau of marvels, the center of good taste, wit, and gallantry.*
Mascarille: *For my part, I maintain that outside Paris there is no salvation for people of breeding.*

—Molière
Two Precious Maidens Ridiculed, 1659

Boussod, Valadon & Co., after a painting by J. L. Gerôme: *Louis XIV and Molière dining at court*, c. 1670. Library of Congress Prints and Photographs Division, Washington, D.C.

By the time of his death, the playwright Molière (Jean-Baptiste Poquelin) had managed to mock most of Parisian high society, bring heaven and hell to the Tuileries, and see himself accused of various immoral acts—including marrying his own daughter.

This may never have occurred had he followed in his father's footsteps and become a *tapissier du roi*. But after a brief stint caring for the king's linens, the young Parisian instead chose to embark on an acting career.

Molière was first a part of L'Illustre Théâtre, a theater troupe unable to live up to its boastful name. Instead, its members, wracked with debt, escaped to the provinces. They would have to wait more than a decade for another chance to prove themselves in Paris.

During its eleven-year absence from the capital, L'Illustre Théâtre built a name for itself. Much of that recognition was due to Molière, who had begun writing farces to accompany the long, sober tragedies performed by the troupe. Molière moved the genre beyond the conventional trapdoors and contrived denouements that characterized most farce; his works became known for their insight into man's vanity and hypocrisy.

In 1659, the troupe was called on to perform for twenty-year-old Louis XIV. The king was then living in his residence at the Louvre, and had L'Illustre Théâtre perform in a ground-floor room, the Salle des Gardes (today the Salle des Caryatides, which houses Roman antiquities). The king was delighted with Molière's farce and granted the troupe the use of the royal court, the Petit-Bourbon, along the extended Cour Carrée of the Louvre.

It was at the Petit-Bourbon, and later at the Palais-Royal, that Molière presented Paris—so accustomed, then, to serious tragedy—with great farce and satire. The first big success came on November 18, 1659, with the premiere of *Two Precious Maidens Ridiculed*. The play satirized the manners of Parisian salons, which had sprung up in private homes in the early seventeenth century in reaction to the deterioration of courtly conversation into vulgar, common speech. Women arrived in elaborate hairstyles and powdered faces, joining male guests (often bedecked in feather hats) to discuss morals, literary works, and grammar. The conversation was

9

filled with excessively refined, lengthy discourse about love and morality.

The nobility and the bourgeois rarely fared well in Molière's works. While he exalted the king, whose reign he linked to France's new era of reason and rationality, he mocked the court's sycophantic behavior.

Molière wrote several plays for the king, and his ballet, *Psyche* (1671), co-written with Pierre Corneille, cost Louis XIV hundreds of thousands of *livres* in order to outfit a room of the Tuileries with wave machines, river gods, a rocky desert, hell, the heavens, and a chorus of 300 divinities standing on cloud machines. A more modest version later ran at the Palais-Royal and was one of the theater's most successful productions.

Had some of Molière's plays been performed a few decades earlier, they might have severed his connections with high society. But a new atmosphere reigned in the capital, which was now flourishing and at peace under Louis XIV. Lighthearted farce could exist alongside the sober tragedies of Corneille and Jean Racine. It was said that all of the members of the salon of

Charles Le Brun: *Portrait of Molière*, 1660.

the Hôtel de Rambouillet—one of the most fashionable salons of its time—turned out to see *Two Precious Maidens Ridiculed*.

Although some members of the nobility did not take well to Molière's work, his greatest enemies were rival theater companies. He was often subject to accusations of plagiarism, as well as attacks on his personal life. In 1662, after living for twenty years with Madeleine Béjart, one of the actors of L'Illustre Théâtre, Molière ended his relationship with her and married her daughter, Armande, who some claimed was his daughter. Armande offered little support to her husband as he coped with these attacks. She did not love him and made little attempt to hide her various trysts, which are believed to have included Corneille and Racine.

In October 1672 Molière moved to his final home at 40, rue de Richelieu, close to the present site of the Comédie-Française. It was there that he wrote *The Imaginary Invalid*, whose character Argan—"blowing his nose, coughing, spitting . . . in a bad mood, tiring people without cease"—was in fact a self-portrait. In the play, Argan, played by Molière, sits in a chair and pretends to be dead in order to test his family's love.

The play opened at the Palais-Royal in February, and on its fourth night Molière began to cough up blood on stage. When the curtain fell, he was rushed back to his home on rue de Richelieu, where he died that night.

Sites

The Pont Neuf

(1st arr.)
Métro: Pont-Neuf

The Les Halles area of Molière's childhood was a bustling, malodorous commercial quarter full of small streets and horse-driven carriages. His father's home, then at 96, rue St.-Honoré, was across the street from the Croix-du-Trahoir fountain, where the condemned were brought to be mutilated or hung. A few blocks away was the Louvre palace, then under construction, while even closer to home was St.-Eustache, the site of Molière's baptism.

Just a short walk from his home was the Hôtel de Bourgogne, Paris' oldest theater and where Molière saw his first production. But it was not in this distinguished setting that Molière developed his comedic talents but at the nearby Pont Neuf. There Molière found a lively street culture far removed from the refined homes around the rue St.-Honoré. Along the bridge's parapets were the *boquinistes*, who sold old books as well as subversive, anti-government pamphlets. At the north end of the bridge, hucksters stood on

makeshift stages to hawk their magic
potions and cures.

Observing and occasionally aiding
these charlatans taught Molière to
contort his body, make strange expres-
sions, and, above all, win over a crowd.
According to legend, he once played a
snakebite victim cured by a charlatan's
antidote. When critics disdainful of
farce and satire wished to attack
Molière, they referred to him as
l'écrivain du Pont Neuf (the writer
of the New Bridge).

Site of the Jeu de paume des Mestayers

12, rue Mazarine (6th arr.)
Métro: St.-Germain-des-Prés

In 1643, Molière formed a theater
group with other young bourgeois, who
proudly called themselves L'Illustre
Théâtre. They rented a covered
tennis court, the Jeu de paume des
Mestayers along the rue Mazarine in
the suburb of St.-Germain-des-Prés.
Eventually the whole troupe moved into
a house next to the theater. (Today the

Flemish school: *The Pont Neuf and the Seine
downstream*, c. 1633.
Musée de la Ville de Paris, Musée Carnavalet. Giraudon/Art
Resource, NY.

only memory of either site is a plaque recalling Molière's time there.)

L'Illustre Théâtre soon encountered problems. As one critic observed, the troupe was little more than a group of amateurs playing in second-rate tragedies, its stars consisting of a hunched, bowlegged man unfit to play tragedy (Molière), a stutterer (Joseph Béjart), and a vulgar redhead (Madeleine Béjart).

Its location in the then-suburb of St.-Germain did little to attract patrons, who mostly lived in the neighborhood between the Marais and the Louvre. Hoping to resolve this problem, L'Illustre Théâtre found a new tennis court, the Croix-Noire, located on the Right Bank of the Marais, between the quai des Ormes and the rue des Barres (where Molière himself would soon move).

But problems continued to plague the troupe, and its members soon found themselves selling their clothes to escape creditors' wrath. By April of 1645, the theater was closed and the troupe was left with few options but to leave Paris and try its luck in the provinces.

Comédie-Française

2, rue de Richelieu (1st arr.)
T: 01 44 58 15 15
Métro: Palais-Royal–Musée du Louvre
www.comedie-francaise.fr

When *The Impromptu of Versailles* was performed for Louis XIV in 1663, Molière took advantage of his audience with the king to attack the other two theaters in Paris—the Hôtel de Bourgogne and the Théâtre du Marais—which he had decided were responsible for many of the attacks on his character.

Soon, the three theaters were exchanging barbs from their respective stages, the Hôtel de Bourgogne going so far as to write its own play, *The Response to the Impromptu of Versailles* or *The Vengeance of the Marquis.*

Ironically, the three feuding troupes fused a few years after Molière's death, when Louis XIV created the Comédiens-Français (soon to become the Comédie-Française) in 1680. Although the troupe operated for many years at 14, rue de l'Ancienne Comédie, its final home was near Molière's last residence along the rue de Richelieu: the southwest wing of the Palais-Royal, which was constructed between 1786 and 1790. Since 1799, Molière's legacy has lived on in this

building. While other French theaters ring three times before a play begins, the Comédie-Française rings six in memory of the fusion of Paris' three original troupes.

The Comédie-Française is the West's oldest theater company, and the building—also known as the House of Molière—is classified as a historic monument. Its interior is a tribute to France's great dramatists, whose busts sit under rows of gilded chandeliers. In the lobby is a relic of France's most famous playwright—the chair in which Molière played Argan, his final role, and where he sat just hours before his death.

L'Auberge du Mouton-Blanc

40, rue d'Auteuil (16th arr.)
T: 01 42 88 02 21
Métro: Église d'Auteuil

Before Molière had a falling out with the tragedian Jean Racine, the two met occasionally with the fable writer La Fontaine and the poet and critic Nicolas Boileau at the Mouton-Blanc cabaret.

Their long dinners featured copious wine (Suresnes and Argenteuil were then in fashion), and were often the testing grounds for the writers' new projects. The Mouton-Blanc cabaret is today a restaurant serving traditional French dishes in the chic sixteenth arrondissement.

Nearby is the site of Molière's home in the neighborhood of Auteuil, where in 1677 he rented a first-floor apartment at 62, rue Boileau. He often hosted his friends for dinner there, and one night his guests became so drunk that they decided to commit suicide by jumping into the Seine. Molière was able to stop them, arguing that they should wait until the daytime since a *si beau projet* deserved a large audience.

St.-Eustache
2, rue du Jour (1st arr.)
Métro: Châtelet–Les Halles

Although the reputation of the theatrical world had improved during the seventeenth century, for the most part the church viewed actors as amoral and decadent. Indeed, a church could —and often did—refuse to bury an actor if he did not recant his profession before his death. This was often done in the final days of the actor's life, not so much for religious reasons but to avoid the complications a church's refusal could cause the actor's family.

It is likely that Molière, like other actors, would have renounced his profession had he lived long enough. Instead, he was rushed home from the performance of *The Imaginary Invalid* and died before a representative from St.-Eustache could arrive.

St.-Eustache was particularly unsympathetic toward actors. Just steps away from the Hôtel de Bourgogne, the church was familiar with the troupe's lifestyle and performances. A burial request for Molière was refused, and it was only with the intervention of Louis XIV and the archbishop that Molière was finally buried (albeit at night, with only two priests in attendance). He was taken to the cemetery St.-Joseph off the rue d'Aboukir, which was a part of the St.-Eustache parish. Few knew where Molière was actually buried. His tombstone was in the cemetery's center, which was fitting for someone of his fame, but popular belief was that the church had actually buried his body toward the cemetery's edge, signifying the low regard it held for actors.

In any case, the group that broke into Molière's tomb a century later to save his bones from revolutionary mobs moved the remains inside the St.-Joseph church.

When the Revolution passed, there was talk that Molière's alleged remains would be placed in the Panthéon, but ultimately they were buried in Père-Lachaise. Although the St.-Joseph cemetery was demolished in the nineteenth century, the St.-Eustache church in which Molière was baptized—and whose representatives he fought until his death—still stands.

Voltaire

(1694–1778)

"But, Monsieur Martin, have you seen Paris?"

"Yes, I have seen Paris; it is a mixture of all the species; it is a chaos, a throng where everybody hunts for pleasure and hardly anybody finds it, at least so far as I could see."

—Voltaire
Candide, 1759

"Louis XIV did more for his people than twenty of his predecessors put together," wrote Voltaire (Jean François-Marie Arouet) of the Sun King, who ruled France from 1643 to 1715. Louis XIV ushered in an era in which architecture and the arts flourished in Paris—then the largest city in Europe. During his seventy-two-year reign, the streets were paved, a police force was created, and structures such as the Louvre were erected. The king famously moved the royal court to his new Versailles palace, where he could keep his eye on scheming courtiers and courtesans.

But these laudatory lines from Voltaire's *The Age of Louis XIV* were published in 1751—thirty-six years after the monarch's death—and the throne was now occupied by Louis XIV's great-grandson. The grandeur of the Sun King had been replaced by the blunders of Louis XV; the once austere Versailles court was now known as one of the most corrupt in all of Europe. And Voltaire's appraisal of the life of Louis XIV was not looked upon kindly by the new ruler.

By then Voltaire's reputation as a troublemaker was already firmly established in Paris. In his early twenties he was sent to the Bastille after bragging about his authorship of the poem "Puero Regnante," in which the Regent, the Duke of Orléans, was accused of incest. From May 1717 to April 1718, Voltaire sat comfortably in the infamous prison insulting the Regent and reading Homer.

He was back in the Bastille in 1726 after unwisely directing a witty insult toward a chevalier with a powerful family. He was released after promising to exile himself in England, and while there for three years kept at his anti-clerical texts. The provocative works would have landed him in jail yet again, but he fled Paris before he could be arrested and took refuge in the Cirey country home of Émilie du Châtelet, his mistress. (She is believed to have authored a 738–page analysis of the errors in the Book of Genesis.)

But Voltaire was a social man and was often drawn to the capital to see his friends. He drank coffee with the playwright Alexis Piron at Le Procope in the Latin Quarter and played chess at the Café de la Régence on the rue St.-Honoré. He was also frequently invited to the various dinners and salons held by his wealthy friends.

Voltaire's social life was compromised by an increasingly hostile church and the court of Louis XV. Although he was never officially exiled from the capital, it was clear he was unwelcome. He avoided Paris in his later years and, after editing Frederick the Great's French poetry in Prussia, settled first near Geneva, then in the small French town of Ferney. He was now extremely wealthy and enjoyed the same luxuries as the bourgeois he mocked in his works.

Voltaire spent his twenty-three years of exile from the capital composing pamphlet after pamphlet designed, in his words, to *écraser l'infâme!*—crush the vile thing!—namely, superstition and religion. It was also in exile in 1759 that he composed his celebrated mockery of optimism and religion, *Candide*.

At age eighty-four Voltaire decided to return to the capital. The newly crowned Louis XVI chose not to object to Voltaire's arrival in 1778, while the rest of Paris—from Marie-Antoinette to Benjamin Franklin—enthusiastically feted his return. His play *Irène* was received that year at the Comédie-Française to thunderous applause. At one performance, the audience encouraged the actors to

place a crown of laurels upon Voltaire's head, proclaiming him the French Sophocles. The public accompanied his carriage to his home at 27, quai des Théatins, and one enthusiastic fan replaced the plaque for "quai des Théatins" with "quai de Voltaire" (the change was officially accepted in 1791).

It was on the second floor of this home, which still stands, that the dying Voltaire agreed to the visit of emissaries from St.-Sulpice. The church hoped that in his final moments one of the Enlightenment's greatest figures would recant and recognize the divinity of Jesus Christ. Instead, before turning his back on them, Voltaire replied:

"In God's name, don't mention Him to me!"

Sites

Hôtel de Sully

62, rue St.-Antoine (4th arr.)
T: 01 44 61 20 00
www.archivesnationales.culture.gouv.fr/arn
Métro: St.-Paul

In 1725, Voltaire was dining at the stately Marais mansion of the Duke of Sully when a servant came in with the message that Voltaire was requested below—someone had important information about a plot against him.

Unknown to Voltaire, the mysterious visitor was the chevalier Guy-Auguste de Rohan-Chabot, who had recently insulted Voltaire for having adopted a pseudonym rather than use his real name, Jean François-Marie Arouet. Voltaire later retorted, "I am the first of my name and you are the last of yours."

When Voltaire reached the door of the Hôtel de Sully, two men asked him to approach a waiting carriage, in which the chevalier was waiting. As Voltaire moved away from the gate of Sully's mansion, the chevalier's lackeys began to hit him with sticks.

After his beating, Voltaire vowed revenge and took up fencing. But before a duel could take place, Voltaire was taken to the Bastille under a *lettre de cachet* signed by one of the chevalier's powerful relatives.

The site of Voltaire's beating, the Hôtel de Sully, today houses France's National Archives. Visitors traverse a long garden before passing below the two sphinxes that guard the main entrance to the seventeenth-century building. Sections of the mansion were dismantled and sold during the French Revolution, but it was bought and restored by the government following World War II.

Hôtel Lambert

1, quai d'Anjou (4th arr.)
The building is closed to the public.
Métro: Pont-Marie

One of the most impressive reminders of Voltaire's time in Paris is the luxurious Hôtel Lambert on the Île St.-Louis. Although the mansion had been purchased by Voltaire's mistress, Émilie du Châtelet, the two spent little time there. Émilie did her best to keep Voltaire away from Paris's distractions by keeping him at their country home in Cirey, where the two pored over Newton and philosophy. "Only in the country may I hold his imagination in check. Sooner or later in Paris I'd lose him," she wrote to her friend the Duke of Richelieu in 1735.

The Hôtel Lambert was one of many houses on the seventeenth-century quai d'Anjou constructed by Louis Le Vau, the famous architect who would later build the enormous château of Vaux-le-Vicomte for Louis XIV's finance minister, Nicolas Fouquet.

Voltaire delighted in its extravagance, much of which was owed to the decorator of Versailles, Charles le Brun. Its drawing rooms, the *cabinet de l'amour*, and the *cabinet des muses* were adorned with painted panels depicting muses, mythical gods, and ancient ruins by Eustache Le Sueur and Pierre Patel. (Many of these panels today hang in the Louvre.)

The entrance, guarded by two bronze lions, is at 2, rue St.-Louis-en-l'Île, but the best view of the façade is from the quai d'Anjou or from the Sully Bridge. Nearby is a plaque marking the water level of the flood of Paris in January 1910, and at no. 17 is another Le Vau project, the Hôtel Lauzun, once home to the poet Charles Baudelaire.

Académie Française

23, quai de Conti (6th arr.)
Métro: Pont-Neuf or St.-Michel
www.academie-francaise.fr

"It would be a disgrace for the Academy if he were in it, and some day it will be ashamed of not inviting him."

The opinion of Voltaire held by the philosopher Montesquieu was shared by many members of the Académie Française. Founded in 1653 by Cardinal Richelieu, the academy was an organization of forty men of letters whose mission was to establish official rules of the French language. Election to one of its seats promised great respect, and these men were known as *les immortels*. Voltaire's election in 1746 was not so much out of respect for the author as it was in recognition of the high position he then held in King Louis XV's court.

In the following decades, Voltaire's provocative texts did little to raise him in the esteem of most of his colleagues. When the academy honored him in a ceremony near the end of his life, more than half of *les immortels* refused to attend. But Voltaire was in a conciliatory spirit that day and stuck to innocent topics. Among them, he proposed that the academy undertake the creation of a new, definitive dictionary of the French language, with great attention paid to etymology, citations, and the conjugation of verbs. He even offered to contribute the letter "A."

The Académie Française has retained its influence over the centuries, and even the most well-known French writers—Victor Hugo, Honoré de Balzac, and Charles Baudelaire, among others—went to great lengths in the hopes of winning a spot among the select.

Le Procope

13, rue de l'Ancienne-Comédie (6th arr.)
T: 01 40 46 79 20
www.procope.com
Métro: Odéon

In the eighteenth century, those hoping to see a work by Voltaire headed to 14, rue de l'Ancienne-Comédie in the Latin Quarter, then the home of the Comédie-Française (today located near the Louvre). The theater was just steps away from Le Procope, the choice meeting spot for playwrights, artists, and fashionable Parisians.

Opened in 1686 as Paris's first café-glacier, Le Procope soon gained fame for its sorbet and coffee. But it was the café's proximity to the theater that won it a loyal following among the literary crowd, which included Voltaire, La Fontaine, Rousseau, and Pierre Beaumarchais and, in the next century, Honoré de Balzac, Victor Hugo, Paul Verlaine, and Oscar Wilde. Diderot and d'Alembert's Encyclopédie was born here, and Benjamin Franklin is said to have revised the US Constitution at one of its tables. Robespierre, Danton, and Marat dined there in the days leading up to the French Revolution.

Le Procope has survived Paris's turbulent history, hidden away from the Latin Quarter's noisy main streets on a narrow cobblestone passageway. Souvenirs of its most famous regulars —including Voltaire's regular table— are on display on both floors of Le Procope.

Panthéon

Place du Panthéon (5th arr.)
Open in the winter, Monday–Friday 10am–5:30pm; summer, Monday–Friday 9:30am–6:30pm
Closed on holidays.
Métro: Cardinal Lemoine

Voltaire called Jean-Jacques Rousseau "the enemy of mankind." "That wretched man," countered Rousseau, "has corrupted my country."

"One feels like crawling on all fours after reading your work," wrote Voltaire in 1761 to Rousseau, who spoke out against social inequalities and famously urged men to head "back to nature." One year after receiving the letter from his wealthy rival, Rousseau published The Social Contract (1762). The text, which preached that all men were born equal, is often considered the precursor to the French Revolution. To Voltaire, however, Rousseau's philosophy was little more than passionate sentimentality clouding reason and rationality.

For the past three centuries, a statue of Voltaire has stood directly facing that of Rousseau in the crypt of the Panthéon. Neither body, however, now lies in its tomb. Following the collapse of Napoleon's empire in 1814, the Panthéon was raided and the remains of two of the eighteenth century's most important thinkers were carried off. However, the standing figures sculpted by Jean-Antoine Houdon remain above both philosophers' tombs.

Anonymous (17th century): Coronation of Voltaire at the Théâtre Française.
© Erich Lessing/Art Resource, NY.

The Marquis de Sade

(1740–1814)

The passions, you see, acquire force

beneath the ascetic; the monastic

life nurtures the seeds; Paris would

only dissipate my energies and

eventually taint the strength and

purity of my desires.

—The Marquis de Sade
Juliette, 1797

The Marquis de Sade (Count Donatien-Alphonse-François de Sade) came to Paris at age thirty-six not as a writer but as a criminal. His outrages up until then were many: he had celebrated Easter Sunday by flagellating a woman he had locked up in his home; he had been accused of poisoning and sodomy in Marseille; and at his estate in Lacoste he had established a small harem (and allegedly a garden full of human bones).

But it was not for any of these acts that in 1777 Sade was thrown into the prison in the Bois de Vincennes, and then the Bastille. Rather, he was imprisoned under a *lettre de cachet*—a letter affixed with the royal seal, guaranteeing his indefinite imprisonment. The request had been submitted by Sade's powerful mother-in-law, Madame de Montreuil, a jealous woman infatuated with her daughter's husband.

Sade claimed he was a libertine, not a criminal, and did not deserve such punishment. But under the *ancien régime*, no reason or proof was needed to obtain a *lettre de cachet*, and an individual had no means of recourse in the courts of law. Sade was taken to the Château de Vincennes, a medieval fortress whose large moats, thick walls, and small windows had made it easy to convert into a prison in the sixteenth century.

In his sixth year of imprisonment at the Château de Vincennes, where he was "locked up behind nineteen iron doors, like a wild beast," Sade turned to writing as a means of escape. After writing hundreds of letters and a handful of plays, he embarked on *The 120 Days of Sodom*, whose tortures and debaucheries were far more scandalous than any of the marquis' own. The novel was, in one part, a mockery of contemporary Paris, where, despite the era of supposed enlightenment begun during Louis XIV's reign, public tortures and punishments still drew large crowds. The four powerful, merciless libertines in Sade's work—including one who is a "pillar of society"—commit abusive acts at their weekly supper parties in Paris.

The libertines decide to round up several women, men, boys, and girls and leave Paris for a remote Gothic castle in the Black Forest. For 120 days they engage in various acts of torture, sacrilege, and murder in the belief that "man can aspire to felicity only by serving all the whims of the imagination." The book waged war against society and its values, and Sade aimed "to outrage the laws of both nature and religion." (Sadism—the love of cruelty—was derived from Sade's name.)

Long before Sade reached the 120th day of torture he set aside his novel and instead began an epistolary work, *Aline and Valcour* (1795), which alluded to problems growing in Paris. It was now 1786, just three years before the outbreak of the French Revolution. Although Sade had been cut off from French society for almost a decade, he was well aware of the turmoil in the streets below.

In September of 1788, Sade requested new quarters and was moved to a sixth-story cell in the Bastille overlooking the rue St.-Antoine—the heart of revolutionary activity in both eighteenth- and nineteenth-century Paris. By the winter, riots had broken out, and Parisians were congregating near the Bastille, where the cannon was kept loaded in the event of an attack. On July 2, 1789, Sade sat in his cell and took hold of the long tin pipe he had been given to dispose of urine and water out his window. He used the pipe as a megaphone and shouted down to the street. Soon a crowd gathered, and Sade appealed to them for help. The prisoners, he said, were being slaughtered.

Deemed a security threat, Sade was transferred to the asylum of Charenton, five miles outside Paris. In the rush, his belongings were left behind at the Bastille. Ten days later, 900 people stormed the prison in search of the Bastille's store of gunpowder—the French Revoluton had begun. Until his death, Sade mistakenly believed *The 120 Days of Sodom*—and scores of other tales and plays—had been destroyed.

In March 1790, prisoners held under *lettres de cachet* were liberated and Sade, now nearly fifty, was a free man. The revolution soon turned bloody. In January of 1793, King Louis XVI was executed. The ensuing Terror would see 30,000 people killed, sometimes over as little as a neighbor's denunciation. Sade, now president of one of Paris's forty-eight sections, had the power to be as cruel as he wished but wanted none of it. As one of his libertines had said in *The 120 Days of Sodom*, "the idea of evil is more exciting than the fact of libertinage."

The realities of the guillotine were too much for Sade, who had seen such tortures only in his imagination. He resigned from his post and, in his new role as vice president, undertook more

agreeable tasks, such as renaming Parisian streets with patriotic names (e.g., rue de l'Homme Libre).

His life came under threat twice during the Revolution. Jean-Paul Marat, a leader of the bloody, extremist Jacobins, had read of Sade's libertine past and in June 1793 mistakenly denounced the Marquis de *la Salle* in his paper, *L'Ami du Peuple*. But before Marat could set the record straight, he himself fell victim—while in the bathtub—to an assassin, Charlotte Corday. The unfortunate Marquis de la Salle—not Sade—was executed.

Later that year, Sade was arrested and denounced for "moderatism," or not being sufficiently radical in his revolutionary activities. He ended up at a prison hospital at Picpus (near place de la Nation), whose garden was soon uprooted to hold the bodies of the guillotined. (The guillotine had been moved from place de la Concorde to the place de la Nation in June 1794 after residents complained of the putrid smell.)

Picpus, Sade wrote, was "an earthly paradise—beautiful house, superb garden, choice company, pleasant women. But suddenly there was the place of execution positively under our windows and the middle of our beautiful garden became a cemetery for the victims of the guillotine."

Sade was to be executed on July 24, 1794, but he had been moved so many times that the bailiff could not find him, and he was spared.

"Imprisonment by the nation, with the guillotine under my eyes, did me a hundred times more harm than all the Bastilles you could imagine," he wrote.

In his time, Sade's novels sold well, but the editions were clandestine and he earned no profit. Nevertheless, he was deemed responsible for the books' existence and thrown into jail once again in March 1801. His final home was a lunatic asylum. The treatment he received was generally much better than that at the Bastille: his mistress was allowed to move in with him, and he participated as a writer and an actor in the asylum's balls and performances. The events attracted many curious Parisians, and soon Sade was feasting in his room with celebrated actors and actresses.

He died in 1814, still imprisoned—the existence that had become the most familiar to him.

Anonymous: *Portrait of Marquis de Sade.*
Bibliothèque Nationale, Paris, France. Giraudon/Art Resource, NY.

Sites

Château de Vincennes

1, avenue de Paris
T: 01 48 08 31 20
Open April 1–September 30,
10am–12 pm and 1:15–6pm;
October 1–March 31,
10am–12pm and 1:15–5pm
www.chateau-vincennes.fr
Métro: Château de Vincennes

"I am in a tower, enclosed behind nineteen doors of iron and receiving daylight only through two small windows with a score of bars on each. For ten or twelve minutes each day I have the company of a man who brings me food. The rest of the time I spend alone, and weeping," complained the marquis during the first month of his imprisonment at the Château de Vincennes.

One of France's twenty state prisons, the Château de Vincennes was a medieval fortress whose dungeon had been converted into a prison during the sixteenth century. A prisoner hoping to escape would first need to slip past the three bolted doors of his cell, then the triple-gated entrance at one of the building's corners, and finally through the outer wall, which was made up of three gates that required at least two men to open.

Sade's stay at Vincennes lasted nearly seven years. It was interrupted in 1788 by a trip to Aix, where Sade defended himself from accusations of having poisoned and sodomized four prostitutes while in Marseille. (The "poison" was Spanish Fly, also known as *pastilles de Richelieu*, because of the Duke of Richelieu's frequent use of the pill in his own acts of debauchery.) Although Sade was cleared of the charges at Aix, he knew he was to be returned to Vincennes to serve the remainder of his other sentence under the *lettre de cachet*. He escaped briefly but was found one month later at his château in Lacoste and dragged back to Vincennes. Sade soon complained to the guards that he was being devoured by rats and mice: "When I ask for a cat to be put into the neighboring room, they say, 'Animals are prohibited.' To which I reply: 'You are such fools! If animals are prohibited, so should rats and mice be.'"

He spent the next five years obsessing about revenge and devising wild numerology schemes that would reveal to him the length of his stay. ("This letter has 72 syllables which are the 72 weeks still to go. It has 7 lines plus 7 syllables, which are exactly the 7 months and 7 days there are from 17 April to 22 January 1780," he wrote in an analysis of one of the letters he had received.)

In his sixth year of imprisonment he turned his energy to writing, the passion that would most occupy him once he was transferred to the Bastille in 1784.

Place de la Bastille

(4th arr.)
Métro: Bastille

When the Château de Vincennes was closed as a prison in 1784, Sade was transferred to another fortress turned prison: the Bastille. Located about three miles away, it faced the working-class area known as the Faubourg St.-Antoine. He was allowed to take nothing with him, and his books and manuscripts—including the *The 120 Days of Sodom*—were left behind.

Sade was escorted to one of the Bastille's towers, where he was shown to a fifteen-foot-diameter cell on the second floor. He was one of twelve prisoners over whom fifteen warders kept watch.

Although it was much smaller than his previous cell, Sade soon had a few comforts, including his books and several fresh writing notebooks sent on by his wife. He was surprised to see that his manuscript for *The 120 Days of Sodom* had been sent on as well—a fortuitous act of carelessness on the part of the prison censor.

Sade anticipated further censorship and surveillance while at the Bastille, and when he reached the thirtieth day of *The 120 Days of Sodom*, he stopped work and began to make an easy-to-hide copy of his manuscript. For one month he wrote in microscopic print on thin sheets of paper only five inches wide. When he finished, the scroll amounted to thirteen yards and contained not only the first thirty days of tortures but also notes on revisions and how he should proceed for the next ninety days. It was this manuscript that survived the storming of the Bastille.

Stones from the Bastille prison can now be seen in the subway station that runs below the place de la Bastille. Aboveground, the prison has been replaced by the Colonne de Juillet, erected following the overthrow of Charles X in July 1830. Each July 14, the French gather here in honor of Bastille Day, which marked the beginning of the French Revolution.

Le Théâtre Molière

Passage Molière
157, rue St.-Martin (3rd arr.)
T: 01 44 54 53 00
www.maisondelapoesie-moliere.com
Métro: Rambuteau or Châtelet–Les Halles

Built in 1791, Le Théâtre Molière was a new theater in the small passage between the rue St.-Martin and the rue Quincampoix, just steps from the modern Centre Pompidou. It was known for its revolutionary pieces and was the first theater to stage one of Sade's plays. Patriotic audience members occasionally disrupted the plays in order to make political proclamations or voice disagreement with the playwright.

"Murmurs arose. . . . During the second scene, the noise increased; during the third, it reached its highest pitch; during the fourth, the actors left the stage," reported the *Journal des théâtres*, following the debut of Sade's *The Suborner* in 1791 at Le Théâtre Molière, shortly after his release from the Charenton prison.

"The members of the audience were at each other's throats," Sade recalled of the second performance. The play was soon suspended.

In Sade's time, the round theater was covered in yellow marble, and three tiers of glass loges reflected the elegance of both the décor and the audience. The theater changed names several times over the next two centuries and by the late twentieth century there was little left of its original appearance other than a few stone columns and a wall inscription reading "We ask that you please leave your weapons and umbrellas at the coatcheck."

In 1974, the city decided to save the building by declaring it a historic monument, and a massive restoration in the 1990s brought back the theater's original architecture and décor. Today the building is also home to the Maison de la Poésie, which houses more than 6,000 works of poetry.

Honoré de Balzac

(1799–1850)

"Aha! my boy, Paris is Paris, and the provinces are the provinces."

—Honoré de Balzac
Lost Illusions, 1837–1843

"Paris, it's just the two of us now!" cried the young student of Honoré de Balzac's *Father Goriot*, as he gazed out onto the city from the heights of the Père-Lachaise cemetery.

The student, Rastignac, had come to Paris from the provinces, hoping to make his fortune through an honest profession. He discovered a city of ruthless and selfish people led astray by greed and ambition. As one Parisian tells him, success in Paris only comes "by the brilliance of genius or by corruption."

Honoré de Balzac made his way in Paris with a bit of both. He arrived as a teenager and soon disappointed his bourgeois parents by announcing his decision to become a writer. They reluctantly agreed to pay the rent for a run-down room near the Bastille, an "open-air sepulcher" where "the disjointed tiles left the sky in view." In exchange, he was instructed to leave his room only at night so that family friends nearby in the chic Marais would not know he was pursuing such a disgraceful profession.

After a brief attempt at playwriting, Balzac further shocked his family by joining a team of writers who produced several popular novels under the pen names Horace de Saint-Aubin and Lord R'Hoone. Balzac considered the novels, full of dashing heroes, beautiful women, and florid language, to be little more than commercial art and he was soon able to leave the work behind. In his early thirties, he published two works of his own—*The Physiology of Marriage* (1829) and *Scenes from Private Life* (1830)—which were partly based on his observations of (and affairs with) noble women.

The short, portly writer could soon be spotted in Paris's literary cafés such as the Café Minerve and the Café Voltaire, both of which have since disappeared but live on in several of Balzac's novels. He became a target for journalists, who often poked fun at his eccentric, ostentatious ensembles, which typically included a mass of gold finger rings, a white waistcoat with coral buttons, and a flamboyant green tailcoat. His apartment near the Paris Observatory at 1, rue Cassini was equally impressive, with walls covered in blue calico. Balzac's years at rue Cassini saw the publication of three of his most famous novels, *The Magic Skin* (1831), *Eugénie Grandet* (1833), and *Father Goriot* (1834).

These novels also established Balzac as an important member of the

growing French Realist movement. In Balzac's works, Parisian sites and addresses became important backdrops used to identify characters and their social milieu. The world he created was a rich microcosm of Parisian society peopled with aristocrats, the bourgeoisie, criminals, and prostitutes.

Balzac's Paris was also a city of class struggle, a world of vice, "a vast pleasure factory," and "the most indulgent city in the world." Balzac was not immune to its temptations: he ran up large bills throughout the city and was often slipping out back doors to avoid his creditors (or the irate husbands of his mistresses).

In 1836, under threat of a jail sentence for overdue bills, Balzac disappeared from rue Cassini to a new apartment at 13, rue des Batailles near Chaillot (today 9, avenue d'Iéna). He hoped that the dilapidated façade and empty first and second floors would trick creditors, but as an extra precaution he rented the room under the fictitious name of "Madame, the Widow Durand." Only by stating a secret phrase—"Apple season has arrived" or "I come with lace from Belgium"— would one be allowed entry into the dark apartment and the third floor. There, an inconspicuous door opened onto Balzac's luxurious quarters, the walls of which were draped in sumptuous veils of muslin.

From the cushions of his white cashmere divan, Balzac could gaze out his windows and "contemplate this ocean of houses" extending from Étoile to the Panthéon. He would occasionally abandon realism in favor of more romantic exaltations of the city's greatness, mystery, and magic. As he wrote in *Father Goriot*:

> *Paris is a veritable ocean; take as many soundings as you like, you will never know how deep it is. Travel round it, describe it, but no matter how systematic your travels or your description, how numerous and eager the explorers of that sea, there will always be some place untouched, some cave unknown, flowers, pearls, monsters, something unheard of, forgotten by the literary divers.*

But Paris was not so enormous as to keep Balzac safe from the police, and in the spring of 1836 he was thrown into jail for having shirked military duty. Preferring to write about criminals rather than live with

them, Balzac borrowed money and quickly obtained a furnished, private cell, where he welcomed friends, ate catered meals, and received flowers and perfume-scented letters from admirers. Although his stay lasted only eight days, he was soon fleeing more aggressive pursuers—his creditors. He hopped from home to home and was afraid to open the door to even his gardener. (The only person he did not need to hide from was his tailor—Balzac had won his favor by making him a character in his novels.)

In need of a new hideaway, he moved in 1840 to Passy, whose quiet village life attracted bourgeois residents fleeing the noise and grime of Paris. There Balzac rented a floor of the house at 19, rue Basse (today 47, rue Raynouard) under the fictitious name of Brugnol. To support the ruse, he hired a maid and conveniently bestowed the noble title of Madame de Brugnol on her. Security was as strict as ever, and visitors to the apartment were required first to ring the door, then to provide a password and ask for the concierge.

It was at his Passy home that Balzac conceived of *The Human Comedy*, a collection of ninety linked novels and novellas and 2,500 characters—roughly one quarter of which emerge in multiple works, often appearing at different stages in their lives. Fueled by countless cups of coffee, Balzac worked furiously on his collection, which includes *Cousin Bette* (1846), *Father Goriot*, and *Lost Illusions* (1837).

"You don't know that there is nothing more demanding than Paris, that it wants you whole, that there is nothing but solitude for a man who works 16 hours a day. . . . So I live in my hole in Passy like a rat," he wrote in 1842 to his Polish lover, the widowed Madame Hanska.

In an effort to draw Madame Hanska from Russia to Paris, Balzac returned to Paris in 1846 and purchased a run-down home on 14, rue Fortunée (now 22, rue Balzac) off the Champs-Élysées. He quickly became consumed with decorating the house, spending his lover's francs on lavish tapestries, crystal, and a chest that once belonged to Elisa Bonaparte— "It's unique, original, and royal!" he cried. When Madame Hanska grew concerned about his decadence, Balzac downplayed his purchases and reminded the religious woman that their new home had an interior door leading directly to Saint Nicholas chapel, which was located just behind the house.

It was to this church, which still stands at the end of rue Balzac, that the author was taken after his death in the spring of 1850. According to legend, his last words were to call for Doctor Bianchon—not his actual doctor but the character he had created in *The Human Comedy*.

Sites

Le Rocher de Cancale

78, rue Montorgueil (2nd arr.)
T: 01 42 33 50 29
Métro: Sentier

Located on the Right Bank, Le Rocher du Cancale was the restaurant of choice for both Balzac and his characters. Count Henri de Marsay in *The Collection of Antiquities* (1839), Philippe in *The Black Sheep* (1842), and Séraphine in *Cousin Bette* all enjoyed their meals at Le Rocher du Cancale. As Balzac described in *Cousin Bette*:

> At half-past six, in the best room of the restaurant where everybody in Europe dined, a magnificent service of silver, made expressly for dinners for which vanity pays the bills in bank-notes, glittered on the table. A stream of light poured in veritable cascades from the edges of the chased metal. Waiters, whom a provincial visitor might have taken for diplomats but for their youth, stood by with all the gravity of men who know themselves to be overpaid.

Previously at 59, rue Montorgueil, the restaurant was closed in 1846 and opened across the street at no. 78 under a new owner. The neo-classical façade of today's Le Rocher du Cancale dates to the mid-nineteenth century, and its wooden beams and five preserved, painted panels recall the restaurant's elegant past. Locals come to enjoy an affordable, casual bistro meal at the restaurant, the second floor of which looks out onto the bustling cobblestone rue Montorgueil.

Maison de Balzac

47, rue Raynouard (16th arr.)
T: 01 55 74 41 80
The house is free and open to the public Tuesday–Sunday, 10am–6pm.
www.paris-france.org/musees/balzac
Métro: Passy, La Muette, or Boulainvilliers

The Maison de Balzac in Passy holds some of Balzac's most treasured possessions, from the author's letters to Madame Hanska to a turquoise-encrusted cane whose extravagance made him the laughingstock of the literary press. Balzac inhabited this three-story home from 1840 to 1847, and it was here that he created *The Human Comedy*.

The house's furniture bears testament to the author's extraordinary output: Balzac's small, wooden writing desk caves slightly in the center from the pressure of his heavy arm moving back and forth as he wrote:

> I possessed it for ten years, it saw all of my misery, wiped away all of my tears, knew all of my projects, heard all of my thoughts; my arm almost wore it out moving back and forth over it as I wrote.

On display nearby is the coffee pot that fueled his long nights of writing.

Balzac was fond of his Passy neighborhood, which had also been home to Benjamin Franklin during the American Revolution. Although the neighborhood was incorporated into Paris in 1860, it still retains much of its nineteenth-century charm, particularly on such cobblestone streets as the nearby rue Berton and rue de l'Ascension.

Rodin's Statue of Balzac

Corner of boulevards Raspail and
Montparnasse (6th arr.)
Métro: Vavin

It would take forty-one years after
Balzac's death before a statue of him
would be erected in Paris. Following
his death, the Société des Gens de
Lettres (Society of Men of Letters),
which he had founded, commissioned
the respected sculptor Henri Chapu to
create his statue. But Chapu died
before finishing his work, and Émile
Zola, then president of the society,
convinced Auguste Rodin to step in.

Rodin threw himself into the project, rereading Balzac's works, traveling
to his childhood home, and asking
Balzac's tailor to make him a coat
to the writer's measurements. His
preparatory work included fifty studies,
fifteen heads, and seven nudes. The
sculpture—originally scheduled to
be unveiled in May 1893—was not
revealed until an exhibition in 1898.
There, the public gazed upon a massive, three-meter-tall Balzac, his mouth
in a roar and his body clothed in the
monk's dressing gown in which he
worked.

"I wanted to show the great worker
who, haunted at night by an idea, rises
to get it down on his work table," Rodin
explained.

While some journalists appreciated
the work, the public was less kind,
calling it a snowman and an obese
monstrosity. The Société des Gens de
Lettres refused the sculpture, and it
was not until 1939—twenty-two years
after the death of Rodin—that it was
placed at the corner of boulevards
Raspail and Montparnasse, where it
still stands.

Cary: *Balzac's house, rue Fortunée* c. 1889.
Photothèque des Musées de la Ville de Paris.

Alexandre Dumas

(1802–1870)

I was therefore sure, finally, of staying in Paris. An ambitious career opened before me, immense and without limits. God had done everything he needed to do; he had, with his Aladdin's lamp, led me into the garden of fairies.

—Alexandre Dumas
Mes Mémoires, 1852–1855

Alexandre Dumas was just twenty years old when he was led by a friend to Paris and its revered theater, the Comédie-Française. He was introduced to the great French actor Talma, who took the aspiring writer's hand and solemnly declared, "Alexandre Dumas, I baptize you poet in the name of Shakespeare, Corneille, and Schiller." With those words, Alexandre Dumas became a Parisian, returning to his provincial town of Villiers-Cotterêts only long enough to quit his notary studies.

Within five years of arriving in Paris Dumas made his literary debut at the same theater. His play, *Henry III and His Court* (1828), was a huge success, and when the curtain came down, Dumas was swarmed by his good friends—the writers Victor Hugo and Alfred de Vigny and other young men whose long hair and vibrantly colored ensembles stood in stark contrast to the more sober attire of traditional theatergoers. The men cheered Dumas' name, hailing him as the new king of French literature, and attempted to throw the busts of the revered "Ancients"—Racine, Corneille, Molière—out the windows of the Comédie-Française.

"Decadence!" railed the *Gazette de France* the next day. "The anarchists of literature have invaded the Seine!" warned *La Pandore*.

The "anarchists" were none other than the supporters of the fledgling Romantic movement, whose birth in France was ushered in by Dumas' *Henry III and His Court* and Hugo's *Hernani* a few weeks later. Coming of age in the years following Napoleon's reign, the Romantics saw only the ills of the restoration of the monarchy. They felt that literature, like man's own existence, should be an expression of creativity, free from rigid rules governing style and subject matter.

This *mal du siècle* manifested differently in each author's works. If Hugo's Paris was one of revolution, and Balzac's one of vice, for Alexandre Dumas it was a magical feast upon which greedy men gorged themselves. In his celebrated revenge tale, *The Count of Monte Cristo* (1844), Paris is a city where everything—status, revenge, and women—"is for sale to him who cares to pay the price."

But it was also a city where outsiders—the Count of Monte Cristo or the provincial boy d'Artagnan of *The Three Musketeers* (1844)—could triumph through skill and wit.

Dumas himself was an outsider and saw in these characters his own rise and success in Paris. He was not only a provincial with little formal education but a quadroon as well: his grandfather, a French marquis, had married a slave from St. Domingo. At well over six feet tall, Dumas cut a striking figure in Paris, with brown, frizzy hair and eyes the press described as the color of sapphires. He was also known as a "Don Juan by night," a reference to his numerous romantic liaisons, which produced several children—including Alexandre Dumas *fils*, who would become a famed author in his own time.

Dumas was welcomed by the Romantics, who admired his fast-paced adventure tales. The men met for dinners at the Arsenal and were often on hand to promote each other's works. When Dumas experienced a lackluster premiere of his play *Christine* (1830), Hugo and Vigny snatched the manuscript from his apartment and spent the night revising it. When Dumas awoke in the morning, he found an improved version of the play on his desk.

They were also united in a common political cause—republicanism— and both Hugo and Dumas were active participants in *Les Trois Glorieuses*, the three-day-long popular uprising of July 1830 that ended the absolute monarchy of Charles X. Dumas fought against the royal troops and conquered the Artillery. The raid soon gave way to pillaging, and Dumas—afraid of what might become of the objects—attempted to save some of the most important, including the shield and sword of François I and the harquebuse (firearm) of Charles IX. He also took François I's armor from the Battle of Marignan and crossed Paris dressed half in Renaissance armor, half in 1830s attire in order to bring it to the safety of his apartment at 25, rue de l'Université. He then returned to the thick of the action, invading the Tuileries with the masses and leading a small troop to distribute gunpowder on the rue Mazarine.

Although *Les Trois Glorieuses* was a bloody revolt, Dumas—like the mighty heros who populated his works—escaped unharmed. His taste for adventure led him across Italy and Switzerland, and later he spent four years alongside the Italian revolutionary Giuseppe Garibaldi.

The exotic landscape of his travels inspired him to try his hand at novels, which by the late 1830s had become a lucrative endeavor thanks to the introduction of serials in newspapers. Dumas' lifelike dialogue, fast-moving and gripping plots, and recurring characters (a technique also employed by Balzac) made him an ideal serial writer, guaranteeing a faithful readership. Dumas also found a way to increase his profits by passing the tasks of research on to collaborators, which allowed him to concentrate solely on the writing.

As he entered his forties, Dumas, like so many of his "outsider" characters, had triumphed in Paris. His vision of the city as a place of great success or failure surfaced in *The Mohicans of Paris* (1854–1859), in which he described the city as a "luminous foyer, which emits the rays that will light the world, illuminating some, setting others ablaze."

Dumas purchased a home in the Parisian suburb of St.-Germain-en-Laye and brought a designer from Tunis to decorate it with arabesques. Later he had a castle built nearby, the Monte-Cristo, which was a mix of Renaissance, rococo, and Gothic architecture. Back in Paris, he built a theater along the boulevard du

Temple—also known as the boulevard du Crime for the several poisonings, murders, and melodramas that occurred in the street's theaters each night. From 1846 until 1850, the Théâtre-Historique produced pieces from all over Europe, as well as from up-and-coming French playwrights and the current works of Dumas' friends.

During those successful years, Dumas kept a tobacco jar full of cash from which his friends helped themselves freely. But such careless attitudes toward money eventually bankrupted him. By the mid-1850s, Dumas was unable to get plays past Louis Napoleon's censors, who were eager to block the works of a known republican and friend of the exiled Victor Hugo. Ever the optimist, Dumas instead single-handedly established and ran several newspapers, including *Le Mousquetaire* and *Le Monte Cristo*.

In his final years, Dumas was full of plans for new books, a new theater, even a new restaurant he wished to found along the Champs-Élysées. He made no secret of his love for good food and wines, and his last work before his death was a food dictionary. He died quietly in December 1870,

away from the spotlight, the news of his death overshadowed by a harsh winter and the imminent siege of Paris by the Prussians. So little was made over Dumas' death that Victor Hugo later said he only learned of it when reading a German newspaper.

In 2001, the remains of Dumas were moved to the Panthéon, where he now rests alongside his old friend Victor Hugo.

Sites

The Arsenal (Bibliothèque de l'Arsenal)

1, rue de Sully (4th arr.)
T: 01 53 01 25 04
Open Monday–Friday 10am–6pm;
Saturday 10am–5pm
www.bnf.fr/pages/collections/
coll_ars.htm
Métro: Sully-Morland

The Arsenal, said Alexandre Dumas, "was better than a palace, better than a kingdom."

The Arsenal was in fact a library, and the home and workplace of Charles Nodier, a writer and promoter of the Romantic movement. In 1824, he was named librarian of the Arsenal, and each Sunday evening opened his home to the leaders of the literary vanguard.

While the Arsenal is now most often visited for its fine collection, the library frequently holds its own salon, "Lundis de l'Arsenal." In honor of Nodier's salon, actors and lecturers meet at the Arsenal to discuss the work of a particular author.

The Catacombs

1, avenue du Colonel Henri Rol-Tanguy
(14th arr.)
T: 01 43 22 47 63
Open Tuesday–Sunday 10am–7pm
www.v2asp.paris.fr/musees/
musee_carnavalet
Métro: Denfert-Rochereau

> Go down even today to the cata-
> combs, walk longer than the duration
> of your torch, and in vain you will have
> made 1000 landmarks, you will not
> find your path back, you will no more
> return from there than does a stone
> thrown into an abyss!

In *The Mohicans of Paris*, a worried
night watchman waits aboveground
for the return of two lovers who have
slipped him a few francs in order to
see the catacombs, Paris's vast sub-
terranean cemetery. "In vain he called,
in vain he descended, in vain he covered thousands of passages of this
necropolis: nothing. . . . So it was
that the catacombs devoured the two
lovers."

The catacombs date back to 1786,
when the pestilent smell emanating
from the Cemetery of the Innocents
in Paris's center prompted the city to
transfer the cemetery's bones to the
unused quarries underneath Paris.
From that time until the end of the
nineteenth century, the quarries were
used to house the bones of several
million Parisians. Running under Paris
for roughly 11,000 square meters,
the passageways are lined with skulls,
bones, revolutionary graffiti, and mor-
bid poetry.

Today the city only allows access
to one well-marked kilometer of passageway. The unassuming entrance
can be found at avenue du Colonel
Henri Rol-Tanguy—formerly known
as the *barrière d'Enfer*. A warning is
engraved into the lintel of the door:
"Stop, this is the Empire of Death!"

The Ball

40, rue St.-Lazare (square d'Orléans)
(9th arr.)
Métro: Place St.-Georges

On March 18, 1833, King Louis-
Philippe gave a lavish costume ball
at the Tuileries. No republicans or
Romantics were welcome, and so
Alexandre Dumas and his friends set
out to plan an equally extravagant
party to which they would invite "all
the artists in Paris."

Dumas' own apartment at 2,
square d'Orléans was too small to host
many guests, so the owner of a neighboring apartment kindly offered his.
The other apartment was large, but
drab, and its white walls hardly suggested an *air de fête*. Something had
to be done.

Three days before the ball, Dumas
went off to hunt venison and hare for
his guests. He left the interior decora-
tion up to fifteen of his artist and illus-
trator friends, who decided to honor
Dumas' various literary and theatrical
guests by covering the walls with
scenes inspired from their recent
masterpieces. Working with distemper
paints—which could be erased the day
after the ball—they soon transformed
the white walls into colorful renditions
of towers and tigers and scenes from
various plays. On two door panels,
symmetrical portraits represented
Victor Hugo and Alfred de Vigny.

Six hours before the ball Dumas'
good friend Eugène Delacroix
appeared. "So?" he said to Dumas.
"What do you want me to dash off over
there?"

Nadar (Gaspard Felix Tournachon): *Interior of
Catacombs, Paris*, 1861.
Bibliothèque Nationale, Paris, France. Archives Charmet/Bridgeman
Art Library.

Without removing his coat, Delacroix got to work, mounting a charcoal sketch onto one of the panels. As Dumas recalled in his memoirs:

> Then, in an instant, and as if a canvas had been split open, we saw appear under his hand a bloody horseman, entirely bruised, completely injured, dragged along by his horse that was bleeding, bruised, and injured as he was. . . . It was marvelous to see: a circle formed around the master, and each one, without jealousy, without envy, had left his own work to come applaud this other Rubens who simultaneously improvised both composition and execution. In two or three hours, it was finished.

With Delacroix's work on the wall, the preparations were complete and the artists could get dressed. Dumas wore a sixteenth-century costume, while those acting in his *Henry III and His Court* arrived in costumes from the play. The opera composer Gioacchino Rossini came as Figaro, while Delacroix dressed as Dante. In his memoirs, Dumas discreetly omitted the costume of his friend Victor Hugo, who attended the ball incognito with his mistress, Juliette Drouet.

The ball was an enormous success, and at one point Dumas estimated the crowd at around seven hundred people. With two orchestras playing in each apartment, guests could begin their steps in one apartment and continue down the hall into the second apartment, where the dance ended in a waltz.

Château de Monte-Cristo

1, avenue Kennedy
T: 01 39 16 49 49
Open April 1–November 1, Tuesday–Friday 10am–12:30pm, 2–6pm; Sunday 10am–6pm; November–March, Sunday 2–5pm. Guided tours on Sunday afternoon.
www.chateau-monte-cristo.com
Train: From Gare St.-Lazare in Paris, take the St.-Nom-la-Bretêche train and get off at Marly-le-Roi, then take bus line 10 towards Marly le Roi, stopping at "Les lampes." From avenue Kennedy, take the first right, Chemin des Montferrand, and follow the marked path.
RER: Take line A to St.-Germain-en-Laye, then take bus line 10 toward Marly le Roi, stopping at "Les lampes." From avenue Kennedy, take the first right, Chemin des Montferrand, and follow the marked path.

> He descended, or rather seemed to descend, several steps, inhaling the fresh and balmy air, like that which may be supposed to reign around the grotto of Circe, formed from such perfumes as set the mind a dreaming, and such fires as burn the very senses . . . disturb you.
> —Alexandre Dumas,
> *The Count of Monte Cristo,* 1845

"Right here you will plot an English park at the center of which I want a Renaissance castle, in front of a gothic pavilion surrounded by water. There are several sources, so you will create waterfalls for me," Dumas instructed his architect, Hippolyte Durand.

The construction of Dumas' Renaissance château outside of Paris began in 1845, with no expense spared. Skilled Tunisian craftsmen built a Moorish salon inside the château, while the sculptor James Pradier was responsible for several of the sculpted façades, which included portraits of Dumas' favorite writers. Above the entrance Dumas had inscribed: "I love those who love me."

And English-style park on the grounds of Monte-Cristo housed a menagerie described by the writer in his work *Adventures with My Pets* (1868): cats, two parrots, a vulture named Jugurtha, three monkeys, ducks, and peacocks, among others. In the center of the park, a neo-Gothic château known as the Château d'If served as Dumas' private office. "Here I own a tiny earthly paradise," Dumas boasted.

"It's the madness of the times of Louis XV, executed in the style of Louis XII," wrote Balzac. "If you could have seen it you would have been crazy about it."

Dumas named the château after his popular novel about Edmond Dantes, a young sailor accused of treason who escapes from prison and discovers the treasures hidden on the island of Monte Cristo. There Dantes builds a lush, underground palace, transforms himself into the mysterious Count of Monte Cristo, and concocts his revenge.

Although the fictional island of Monte Cristo was set somewhere between Corsica and the island of Elba, Dumas' chateau in Le Port Marly mimicked the exotic opulence of Italian grottos and caves.

The entire chamber was lined with crimson brocade, worked with flowers of gold. In a recess was a kind of divan, surmounted with a stand of Arabian swords in silver scabbards, and the handles resplendent with gems; from the ceiling hung a lamp of Venetian glass, of beautiful shape and color, while the feet rested on a Turkey carpet, in which they sunk to the instep.

Dumas maintained an apartment in Paris but he used Monte-Cristo for his *fêtes* and to host his mistresses and guests—many of whom took advantage of his generosity.

In 1849, overwhelmed by debt, Dumas was forced to sell the property. It has since been declared a historic monument and restored to its original condition.

Victor Hugo

(1802–1885)

It is in Paris that the beating of Europe's heart is felt. Paris is the city of cities. Paris is the city of men. There has been an Athens, there has been a Rome, and now there is a Paris.

—Victor Hugo
Appeal to the Prussians,
September 9, 1870

On the opening night of Victor Hugo's *Hernani* (1830), Hugo's band of followers—"bandits," as they were known in the press—turned up in outrageous hats and coats, waiting for more than an hour at the entrance while the theater's annoyed neighbors shouted insults and threw things at them. One of the young men, Honoré de Balzac, was hit with a stalk of cauliflower. Inside, the rowdy group spent their three-hour wait sprawled on the floor, eating and drinking and relieving themselves in corners. When the theatergoers entered later in the evening, they were shocked to discover the state of their elegant theater.

The raucous bandits were the Romantics, a growing group of writers known for their vivid, detailed images and passionate historical dramas. With the premiere of *Hernani,* Victor Hugo became their leader. The play's success won Hugo recognition from the public as well, and his boyhood idol, the renowned writer François-René de Chateaubriand told him, "I am going, Sir, and you are arriving."

The Romantics soon crowded Hugo's home at 11, rue Notre-Dame-des-Champs. The house in the sixth arrondissement (now home to the Notre-Dame-des-Champs subway stop) looked out onto a wild, immense garden, at the end of which was a door allowing direct access to the Luxembourg Gardens. Hugo later made these gardens the setting for Marius's first glimpse of the criminal Jean Valejean and the orphan Cosette in *Les Misérables* (1862).

But Hugo and his wife, Adèle, were soon forced to move since the "bandits" were not welcome by the owner. At 9, rue Jean Goujon, in a simple apartment looking out onto the dome of the Invalides, Hugo began one of his most famous works, *The Hunchback of Notre Dame* (1831).

Like many other of the Romantics, Hugo often used different historical periods, rather than the modern city, as the settings for his novels. In *The Hunchback of Notre Dame,* he returned to medieval Paris. The novel was in many ways a tribute to Paris, which he compared to the Athens of antiquity and described as a *ville qui chante* (a city that sings). Even when criticizing Paris, Hugo preferred evocative panoramas and lyrical prose:

Library of Congress Prints and Photographs Division, Washington, D.C.

Reconstruct in your imagination the Paris of the fifteenth century . . . project distantly, upon an azure horizon the Gothic profile of that old Paris; make its outline float in a wintry mist clinging to its innumerable chimneys; plunge it into deep night . . . reanimate with shadow the thousand sharp angles of its spires and gables and make it stand out, more jagged than a shark's jaw, against the copper-colored sky of the setting sun.

The Hunchback of Notre Dame became an immediate bestseller when it was published in 1831, and its success allowed the young couple—now with four children—to move to a larger house in the Marais at 6, place Royale (now place des Vosges). Hugo moved his mistress, the young actress Juliette Drouet, to a home just a few doors away at 14, place Royale.

The success that Hugo enjoyed in middle age was disrupted by the coup d'état of 1851, in which Louis Napoleon (Napoleon III) declared himself emperor of France. Hugo vociferously opposed the coup, and he became a wanted man. His past honors—Officer of the Legion of Honor, a deputy of the Second Assembly, and

a seat at the Académie Française—did little to save him. With a fake passport he escaped to Brussels, then Jersey and Guernsey, for what was to be a nineteen-year exile.

Exile turned Hugo away from the historical dramas of his past and toward contemporary France. In 1862, he published *Les Misérables*. Much of the book's action was set in Paris's sewers, labyrinthian Les Halles market, and slums, where "the gloomy voice of the people was heard dimly growling." The backdrop was 1832 and revolution was brewing once again in Paris, led by the notorious Faubourg St.-Antoine neighborhood, which was then a poor artisans' quarter by the Bastille:

Something terrible was brooding. Glimpses could be caught of the features still indistinct and imperfectly lighted, of a possible revolution. France kept an eye on Paris; Paris kept an eye on the Faubourg Saint-Antoine. The Faubourg Saint-Antoine, which was in a dull glow, was beginning its ebullition.

It was not until late 1871, the year France entered its Third Republic, that Hugo made his definitive return to Paris, settling at 21, rue de Clichy. Juliette Drouet, who had accompanied him throughout his exile, moved into an apartment one floor above Hugo in the same building, and despite his advanced age, Hugo continued to have other affairs: when *Hernani* returned to the stage at the Comédie-Française in 1877, Hugo managed to seduce the play's famous star, Sarah Bernhardt, who was more than forty years younger.

At seventy-five, Hugo was advised by his doctor to stop his womanizing. Instead, he moved from his fourth-floor apartment to a small house at 130, avenue d'Eylau so as to avoid climbing so many flights of stairs.

The house on avenue d'Eylau was Hugo's last and best-remembered residence in Paris. On his eightieth birthday, admirers came to gaze up at his window, and a few days later, 600,000 people turned out to witness the renaming of the street avenue Victor-Hugo. From that day, until his death on May 22, 1885, his friends would address their letters to him as "Victor Hugo, on his street."

Sites

Maison Victor Hugo

6, place des Vosges (4th arr.)
T: 01 42 72 10 16
The museum is free and open every day but Monday and holidays
10am–5:40pm
Métro: Chemin-Vert, St.-Paul, Bastille

> What enchantment, those evenings at the Place Royale! In the salon at the back, surrounded by an enormous bed of flowers, were young, beautiful and smiling women, magnificently attired and happy to be in the home of the great poet. . . . After that was the large salon, where there was a crowd of men and women among whom one could not find a single banal person. . . . In the dining room, decorated with old arms, an even larger crowd, where one saw the young eager men, coming and going, sometimes writing or drawing on the open scrapbooks— the men of our time who have become famous.
> —Théodore de Banville, *Mes souvenirs*, 1882

All were impressed by the grandeur of the Hugos' home, which occupied the second floor of one of the most elegant mansions on the place Royale, the old-est square in Paris (today known as the place des Vosges).

Victor and Adèle Hugo inhabited the second floor with their children from 1832 to 1848. In 1903—one year after the hundredth anniversary of Hugo's birth—the city of Paris inaugurated Hugo's former residence as the Victor Hugo museum.

The museum traces Hugo's life from his early childhood in the Feuillantines to his final years on the avenue d'Eylau. Visitors can wander through the salon once frequented by Balzac, Dumas, and the Romantics, as well as artists such as David d'Angers and the pianist Franz Liszt. Hugo's various awards are on display, as is his writing desk. Among the museum's prized pieces are wooden panels Hugo had made for Juliette Drouet while in exile. The close observer will notice that woven throughout the panels— lavishly covered in images of animals and flowers—are the couple's initials.

La Tour d'Argent

15–17, quai de la Tournelle (5th arr.)
T: 01 43 54 23 31
Métro: Maubert-Mutualité

In 1833, Hugo took his new mistress, Juliette Drouet, to La Tour d'Argent, a restaurant whose history dated back nearly three hundred years.

Over dinner, Victor read Juliette the final act of his latest work, *Lucrèce Borgia*, which was based on the true story of an Italian noble woman accused of poisoning her family's rivals. Hugo, overcome by his excitement, could not help but raise his voice as he read the play's most famous line:

"Sirs, you are all poisoned!"

Waiters rushed to reassure the frightened diners.

The elegant top-floor dining room of La Tour d'Argent looks out over the Seine, onto Notre Dame, the Île de la Cité and the Île St.-Louis. Below, its *cave* holds more than 500,000 bottles of wine, including a rare bottle of Napoleon brandy. (The second bottle in the restaurant's possession was stolen by the American billionaire Pierpont Morgan, who replaced the bottle with a blank check.)

Cathédrale Notre-Dame de Paris

Place du Parvis Notre-Dame (4th arr.)
T: 01 42 34 56 10
Free and open to the public daily 8am–6:45pm; closed Saturday 12:30–2pm. Access to its towers (and a view of the staircase leading to Esmeralda's cell) is limited and is subject to a small fee.
www.cathedraledeparis.com
Métro: Cité

Set in 1482, *The Hunchback of Notre Dame* centers on the plight of the disfigured Quasimodo, a ward of the Notre Dame cathedral assigned to ring its bell.

> The cathedral was not only company for him, it was the universe; nay, more, it was Nature itself. He never dreamed that there were other hedgerows than the stained-glass windows in perpetual bloom; other shade than that of the stone foliage always budding, loaded with birds in the thickets of Saxon capitals; other mountains than the colossal towers of the church; or other oceans than Paris roaring at their feet.

John Claude Nattes: *View of the Pont du Chatelet and Notre-Dame Cathedral*, 1810.
Bibliotheque Historique de la Ville de Paris, Paris, France, Archives Charmet/Bridgeman Art Library.

In Hugo's evocation of the great cathedral, Quasimodo was the sole bell ringer for the fourteen-ton bell. In fact, in the fifteenth century, sixteen men were required to ring the bell, and even during Hugo's time, when its movement was facilitated by a pedal mechanism, eight men were necessary. (Today it runs electrically.)

In contrast, Hugo's description of Esmeralda's cell was precise, situating her site of imprisonment in the north tower:

> In Notre Dame it was a cell constructed over one of the side aisles, under the buttresses and facing towards the cloister, exactly on the spot where the wife of the present concierge of the towers had made herself a garden. . . . It was a chamber some six feet square, with a small window and a door following the slight incline of the roofing of flat stones outside. Several gargoyles with animal heads seemed bending down and stretching their necks to look in at her window. Beyond the roof she caught a glimpse of a thousand chimney-tops from which rose the smoke of the many hearths of Paris.

Hugo's lyrical portrait of Notre Dame inspired new interest in the cathedral, which had suffered a great deal since its completion in 1250 (including defacement during the French Revolution and fire during the Commune). One of those moved by Hugo's tale was the young architect Eugène Emmanuel Viollet-le-Duc, who would eventually effect a massive restoration of the old cathedral.

The Arc de Triomphe
Place Charles de Gaulle (8th arr.)
Métro: Charles de Gaulle–Étoile

Hugo died on May 22, 1885, at the age of eighty-three. His body was first displayed at the Arc de Triomphe, which was draped with black crêpe to mark the somber occasion. It was said that more than two million French citizens took to the street that day to mourn Hugo's death and observe the six-hour funeral procession from the Arc de Triomphe to his final resting place at the Panthéon.

Anonymous: *The Funeral of Victor Hugo, the catafalque under the Arc de Triomphe*, 22 May 1885. Archives Larousse, Paris, France/Bridgeman Art Library.

George Sand

(1804–1876)

See, yonder, the affable, winning, hospitable Parisian, as he was described to you, always in a hurry, always careworn! Tired out before you have seen the whole of this ever-moving population, this inextricable labyrinth. . . .

—George Sand
Indiana, 1832

Rebellion was in Aurore Dupin's blood. Her parents' marriage was unconventional: her father was descended from King Augustus II of Poland; her mother was born in a bird seller's boutique along the Seine. At her grandmother's behest, Aurore was sent to a convent, then encouraged to marry.

By age twenty-six Aurore had left her husband, children, and their country home in Nohant in order to live in Paris. Although still under her husband's guardianship, she made do with a small pension and found ways to economize by adopting men's attire and moving into her brother's apartment along the rue de Seine-St.-Germain. Soon Aurore could be seen with a cigar in her mouth, dressed in a gray overcoat, vest, pants, and hat, with a big wool tie and a pair of boots, discussing philosophy and literature with young journalists and students in the Latin Quarter's bistros.

At the suggestion of the writer Honoré de Balzac, she and her lover, Jules Sandeau, wrote a novel. The advance allowed them the luxury of a new three-bedroom apartment at 25, quai St.-Michel, which looked out onto the Seine and would provide the inspiration for Sand's evocation of Notre Dame, "when a dense fog rises from the Seine and surrounds the bases of the towers and makes them look as if suspended in the sky."

Their novel, *Rose and Blanche*, appeared in December 1831, signed by "Jules Sand." The story, about a woman on the verge of becoming a nun, earned the couple another commission, but Sandeau was uninterested in writing another book. Aurore decided to write the novel herself, but it was impossible for her to publish under her own name since she was still under her husband's guardianship.

So it was that Aurore Dupin disappeared, replaced by the cigar-smoking, pants-wearing George Sand.

Sand's first work was *Indiana*, about a woman's fight to love freely outside the confines of marriage. The book—one of the few Sand would set in Paris—culminates with Indiana and her lover leaving the capital to fling themselves off the cliffs of the Isle of Bourbon. Such overwrought drama appealed to the tastes of the time, and *Indiana* received great acclaim when it was published in 1832. Balzac hailed her as his "glorious confrere."

While Balzac and other Romantic writers were fascinated by Paris, Sand saw the city as a cruel and illusory place that leads people astray. In *Indiana* she wrote:

> *You ill-starred provincial, who have left your fields, your blue sky, your verdure, your house and your family, to come and shut yourself up in this dungeon of the mind and the heart—see Paris, lovely Paris, which in your dreams has seemed to you such a marvel of beauty! See it stretch away yonder, black with mud and rainy, as noisy and pestilent and rapid as a torrent of slime!*

Sand was not as progressive as she appeared. She did not support women's suffrage or their representation in government and protested when, during the birth of the Second Republic in 1848, feminists enrolled her as a candidate for election to the National Assembly. The primary concern of her novels—and in her own life—was a woman's right to freely pursue love.

Although Sand spent most of her life at her country home in Nohant, she made frequent trips to the capital in the 1830s and 1840s in order to see her lover, the pianist Frédéric Chopin, as well as friends such as Balzac and the Hungarian pianist Franz Liszt.

In 1848 an insurrection overthrew King Louis-Philippe, producing the Second Republic. Afire with idealistic visions of a harmonious, socialist society, Sand called herself the "Muse of the Republic" and created a short-lived publication called *La Cause du Peuple*. Her writing expressed a new love of Paris, its fraternal spirit and the unity of its people, who have "gathered in the heart of France, in the heart of the world, the most admirable people in the universe. I went many nights without sleep, many days without sitting down. People are mad, they're intoxicated, they're happy to sleep in the gutters and congregate in the heavens."

The bloody insurrections that followed in the coming years shook Sand from her reverie, and she once again took refuge in Nohant. But she never entirely abandoned Paris, and she made frequent trips to see her plays performed there. While the new generation of writers stared in fascinated horror at their city—a Paris transformed over the previous decade by Napoleon III and Baron Haussmann—Sand found its streets harmonious, its wide boulevards "eminently safe," and its citizens united in a common cause.

Sites

19, quai Malaquais

(6th arr.)
Métro: St.-Germain-des-Prés

Henry James once remarked that Sand exhibited no gentlemanly behavior toward her lovers. And in fact, well before she ended her relationship with Jules Sandeau, she met Alfred de Musset, the handsome poet with whom she was to embark on a new affair. Musset moved into Sand's new 19, quai Malaquais apartment around the time Sand's *Léila* (1833) appeared in bookstores. It was this same apartment where, at nineteen and newly arrived in Paris, she had first taken her manuscript to the editor Henri de Latouche, who had taken one look at the piece and declared, "I don't see in this book any element of success; believe me, try going back to your conjugal roof!"

Musset had a wild reputation: his use of opium and alcohol was excessive, and he occasionally suffered from hallucinations. Sand kept to a strict writing schedule and occasionally had to work behind closed doors so as to avoid his advances.

Deciding they could live neither together nor apart, Sand and Musset decided to kill themselves in the Fontainebleau forest outside of Paris— a plan that did not come to fruition. Later, Sand chopped off her long, black hair and sent it to Musset. On another occasion, Musset grabbed a knife, threatened Sand, and then tried to turn it on himself. In 1835, Sand left Paris —as she would do many times over the coming decades—to take refuge in Nohant. She would later give her version of the breakup with Musset in *She and He* (1859).

The 19, quai Malaquais building was also home to the writer Anatole France, whose time there is commemorated by a plaque.

5, 9 square d'Orléans
(9th arr.)
Entry at 80, rue Taitbout
Métro: St.-Georges or Trinité

Not all were immediately taken by *la Sand*. "What an unfriendly woman! Is she really a woman?" asked the Polish pianist Frédéric Chopin. The pianist and the novelist had first met in 1836, introduced by Liszt during one of Sand's sojourns in Paris. Sand was equally unimpressed, writing to a friend, "That Chopin, he's a little girl!"

Their second encounter was more favorable. Sand was taken by Liszt to Chopin's apartment at 5, rue de la Chaussée-d'Antin for a private gathering. As Chopin played at the Pleyel piano, Liszt looked on:

> The light concentrated around the piano, and falling to the floor, glided like a spreading wave until it reached and mingled with the fitful flashes of the fire, from which the orange-lined plumes rose and fell, as if some shifting gnomes attracted to this spot by mystic incantations in their own language. . . . Sitting in an armchair was Madame Sand, nervously attentive and graciously subjugated.

Sand pursued Chopin aggressively, and soon the pianist had settled with her at 16, rue Pigalle. There Sand received her many socialist friends; Chopin had little patience for politics. Their social circle widened when they moved in 1842 to a newly constructed apartment building at nos. 5 and 9 of the square d'Orléans. This corner of the 9th arrondissement was home to the writer Alexandre Dumas, the sculptor Antoine Laurent Dantan, and several other artists. Sand and Chopin invited friends such as Eugène Delacroix and Balzac to join in music and readings at the English-style

square, which still stands today. One of Chopin's friends remarked,

> [Sand] rose in a very theatrical way and walked in a very masculine manner across the salon, towards the gleaming chimney. From the pocket of her smock she brought out an enormous trabucco cigar and cried, across the salon: "Frédéric, a fidibus [match]!" Chopin oscillated sweetly towards her with a fidibus.

Chopin's fight with tuberculosis had left Sand, as she said, "a virgin," and Sand's children had never fully accepted Chopin into their family. Sand ended their nine-year relationship in 1847. They saw each other again only once, in March 1848—a little more than a year before Chopin's death—in the same square d'Orléans they had once shared. On his deathbed Chopin spoke often of Sand, but Sand refused to visit him. When she heard of his death, she placed a lock of his hair he had once sent her in an envelope, on which she wrote in English: "Poor Chopin."

Musée de la vie romantique/ Hôtel Scheffer-Renan

16, rue Chaptal (9th arr.)
T: 01 55 31 95 67
The museum is free and open to the public every day except Monday 10am–6pm
www.paris.fr/musees/Vie_Romantique /default.htm
Métro: Pigalle

At the edge of a shady cobblestone alleyway is the Hôtel Scheffer-Renan, once the home and workshop of Dutch painter Ary Scheffer, the art professor to the children of the Duke of Orléans. Scheffer had two workshops built alongside his home—one for his painting and the other for receiving his many guests, who included Liszt, Chopin, and Sand.

Today the Hôtel Scheffer-Renan is known as the Museum of Romantic Life and houses major works connected to the Romantic period in France. Although the museum includes works by Scheffer, its collection focuses primarily on Sand, featuring roughly 170 documents pertaining to her life and works. In addition to various paintings of Sand and Nohant,

famous portraits by Nadar are on display, as are some of Sand's own watercolors and a mold of Chopin's hand by the sculptor Auguste Clésinger.

Musée National Eugène Delacroix

6, rue de Furstenberg (6th arr.)
T: 01 44 41 86 50
The museum is open every day but Tuesday 9:30am–5pm
www.musee-delacroix.fr
Métro: St.-Germain-des-Prés

> Eugène Delacroix was one of my first friends in the artistic world and I'm happy to still be able to count him among my old friends. . . . In my view, he is the master of these times and, in relation to those of the past, he will remain one of the masters in the history of painting.

Sand first met Delacroix shortly after her breakup with Alfred de Musset, and the painter would soon become a regular in Sand's circle.

"He speaks better than I write," remarked Sand, who often confided in the painter and occasionally hosted him in her Nohant home.

In 1857, Delacroix left Sand and his other artist friends living in the Nouvelle Athène quarter of Paris

and moved to the quiet place de Furstenberg in St.-Germain. The move was designed to allow him to be closer to St.-Sulpice, whose chapel he had been commissioned to paint.

The apartment was hidden at the end of a paved courtyard, the access to which was masked by a large door. Such inaccessibility and tranquility was appealing to Delacroix, who had grown quite sick and could no longer receive good friends with the same frequency as in the past.

Delacroix's home became a national museum in 1971 and is now open to visitors. A selection of his works, including engravings he created of Sand, is on display.

Josef Danhauser: *Liszt at the Piano*, 1840.
Nationalgalerie, Berlin, Germany / Bridgeman Art Library

Charles Baudelaire

(1821–1867)

Old Paris is no more. (Ah, truth be told,
Cities change faster than the human
heart!)

—Charles Baudelaire
"Le Cygne," *Les Fleurs du Mal*, 1861

Charles Marville: *Building of avenue de l'Opéra,*
building site of the mound of Moulins near passage
Molière, Paris, 1858–1878.
Musée de la Ville de Paris, Musée Carnavalet. Lauros/Giraudon/
Bridgeman Art Library.

By the mid-nineteenth century, Paris had grown into a thriving commercial center: railroad tracks were being laid down, a new banking system was in place, and industry and textiles were developing rapidly. The emperor, Napoleon III, had come to power in 1851 and promptly entrusted his city to Baron Georges Haussmann. Haussmann's massive renovation of Paris demolished many of the city's winding medieval streets and created wide, tree-lined boulevards lit by modern gas lamps. Paris was to be a clean and gleaming example of modernity—no matter what the cost to its historic buildings and character.

The modernization of Paris, said the poet Charles Baudelaire with disgust, was a "fashionable error." He wrote that the "world is going to end" and removed the hands of his watch so he could have the words "It is much later than you think" inscribed upon its face.

Baudelaire had seen his city transformed before his eyes. As a child, he had grown up on the Right Bank, wandering about the old medieval quarters and narrow streets that still dominated much of Paris. As a young man, his heroes were not men of science and progress but Victor Hugo, Honoré de Balzac, and the Romantics—the rebellious Parisian poets of the first half of the nineteenth century. But by the time Baudelaire published his first collection of poems in 1857, the passion and magic of the Romantics had given way to realistic descriptions of everyday life or a return to classical prose.

As a teenager, Baudelaire was expelled from school for his *très mauvais esprit*, and although he made some overtures toward launching a law career, he spent far more time in the brothels and cafés around the place de l'Estrapade, behind the great Panthéon. At twenty-one, with a healthy inheritance at his disposal, Baudelaire moved to the Île St.-Louis, then a mysterious and solitary quarter whose low rents drew artists and artisans. He dabbled in drugs and spent his money on prostitutes and expensive artwork. His reputation as a dandy was confirmed by the tall hats, wide-collared shirts, and pale pink gloves he wore.

Displeased with his lifestyle, his family took away his inheritance at age twenty-three and gave it to a guardian to manage. Baudelaire was relegated to living on the interest and spent the rest of his life destitute, sneaking from one hotel to another. During his twenties, he established himself as both a journalist and a well-respected art critic, reserving his poetry for private gatherings among friends. He did not publish his poetry collection, *Les Fleurs du Mal*, until 1857, when he was already in his mid-thirties. A second edition, with thirty-five new poems, was published in 1861.

The Paris of *Les Fleurs du Mal* is a sinister place colored by an inhospitable and cruel modernity. Paris's new gas lamps—there were now more than 30,000—are omnipresent. For Napoleon III and Haussmann, the lamps symbolized enlightenment, increased surveillance, and security. But Baudelaire's view suggested a far more intrusive gaze: "Like a darting, blinking, bloodshot eye / The lamp burns red against the dawning sky."

Baudelaire's rich, lyrical verse recalled that of the Romantics, but his dark subject matter, cynicism, and rough, urban vocabulary were new to French literature. Although critics attacked Baudelaire for his filthy language, and six of the book's poems were suppressed for being "profoundly immoral," there were those

who immediately embraced the poet, whom they saw as a necessary *trouble-fête* (spoilsport) among the overwhelming tide of optimism pushing Paris ahead.

Key to his poems was the dislocation brought about by the loss of roots, customs, and history in the face of rapid modernization. Baudelaire's Parisians are "marked by a kind of doomed beauty," their eyes lit by "the horror of boredom." Baudelaire, who changed addresses more than forty times—and whose only constant possession was a portrait of his father—knew of that restlessness. "I'm alone, without friends, without mistress, without a dog, without a cat—there is no one to complain to. I have only the portrait of my father, who is always silent," the poet wrote to his mother in 1861.

The themes of ennui and solitude would be built upon in Baudelaire's unfinished work, *Le Spleen de Paris*, parts of which were published under a different title in 1864. Traditional verse gave way to small prose poems in which the narrator, a "thoughtful perambulating loner," is overwhelmed by Paris. It is a city full of "discordant cries," "screaming, bellowing, howling, a pandemonium of shouts," where

"nothing can be heard but the rumble of a few belated and decrepit cabs. . . . *Horrible vie! Horrible ville!*"

> *You wanted us to sit on the terrace outside the café at the corner of a newly built boulevard which was still littered with rubble but already making a lavish display of its uncompleted splendors. The café glittered all over with lights. The new gas-jets cast their incandescent novelty all round, brightening the whiteness of the walls, the dazzling planes of a multitude of mirrors, the gilt of all the moldings and cornices . . . the nymphs and goddesses balancing baskets of fruits and pates and game on their heads, multicolored pyramid of ices— all history and mythology were exploited in the service of gluttony.*

In 1861, encouraged by the modest success of a second edition of *Les Fleurs du Mal*—and spurred by his constant need for money—Baudelaire made an unsuccessful bid to join the Académie Française. The Academy did not look kindly upon the bohemian poet, who was rumored

Etienne Carjat: *Charles Baudelaire*, c. 1860.
Archives Larousse, Paris, France/Giraudon/Bridgeman Art Library

to own a pair of riding pants made from the hide of his dead father, to have drunk "spiked wine from the skull of a tigress," sadistically plucked out cat's whiskers, and tried to set fire to the Bois de Boulogne.

That same year, Baudelaire suffered a stroke—the result of the syphilis he had contracted in his youth. His health declining, he left in 1864 for Belgium, but found he missed Paris, where he could engage in "that joyful act, the flânerie in front of the boutiques." He returned an invalid in July 1867, having lost the power of speech after another stroke. Before dying at the age of forty-six, the only word he managed to utter was a curse.

Sites

Hôtel de Pimodan/Lauzun

17, quai d'Anjou (4th arr.)
Closed to the public.
Métro: Pont-Marie

One December evening . . . I arrived in a remote quarter in the middle of Paris, a kind of solitary oasis which the river encircles in its arms on both sides as though to defend it against the encroachments of civilization. It was in an old house on the Île St.-Louis, the Pimodan hotel built by Lauzun, where the strange club which I had recently joined held its monthly séance. I was attending for the first time.

It was difficult in the clump of somber buildings along that deserted quay to distinguish the house for which I searched; nevertheless my coachman, perched high on his seat, managed to read on a marble plaque the half-worn, gilded name of the old hotel, the gathering place for the initiates.
—Théophile Gautier, *On the Club des Haschichins*, 1864

Upon entering the Hôtel de Pimodan, Théophile Gautier was greeted by the Club des Haschichins, whose members included Honoré de Balzac, Alexandre Dumas, Eugène Delacroix, and Charles Baudelaire, who in 1843 was living on the building's top floor in a two-room apartment.

Hashish had been discovered in Egypt during the Napoleonic campaign and by the mid-nineteenth century could be purchased in pharmacies. Under a doctor's guidance, the men of the Club des Haschichins were each given a Japanese saucer in which a thumb-sized portion of greenish jam— hashish—had been placed. "This will be deducted from your share in Paradise," the doctor told Gautier, as he handed him his saucer.

Baudelaire's experiences with the notorious Club des Haschichins in his early twenties were the beginning of his exploration of drugs—the *paradis artificiels* of which he would write in *Les Fleurs du Mal*. Fascinated by the effect of drugs on the body and on writing, he authored an 1851 essay, "Comparing Wine and Hashish as Means of Multiplying Individuality." In fact, despite his bohemian reputation, Baudelaire was an infrequent user of hashish and preferred to study the effects of the drug on his friends:

"It sometimes happens that people completely unsuited for word-play will improvise an endless string of puns and wholly improbable idea relationships fit to outdo the ablest masters of this preposterous craft," he wrote, but later concluded that drugs were an insufficient means to attain creativity.

The once notorious Hôtel de Pimodan still stands on the Île St.-Louis, although it is now referred to as the Hôtel Lauzun. A short walk from the mansion is 6, rue Le Regrattier, where Baudelaire often visited one of his early mistresses, the actress Jeanne Dorval. A quadroon known as the *Venus noire*, Jeanne inspired several poems in *Les Fleurs du Mal*, as well as a portrait by Manet. While Dorval and Baudelaire were living on the Île St.-Louis, Le Regrattier was known as the rue de la Femme-Sans-Tête. The street's original name can still be seen, engraved in stone at the beginning of the street.

Hôtel de Voltaire

19, quai Voltaire (7th arr.)
T: 01 42 61 50 91
www.quaivoltaire.fr
Métro: Musée d'Orsay

> Dreary daybreak, quaking in her pink-green gown,
> Inched up the barren Seine. Bleak Paris-town—
> Sullen old workman—rubbed the sleep away, took up his tools, and faced another day.
> —"Crépuscule du matin," *Les Fleurs du Mal*, 1861

The plaque outside the Hôtel de Voltaire bears this poem and another plaque commemorates Baudelaire, who stayed here, along the banks of the Seine, from 1856 to 1859. It was here that he worked on *Les Fleurs du Mal* and on his ongoing translation of the works of Edgar Allan Poe. A few doors down at no. 13 was the *Moniteur Universel*, where Baudelaire would head each night to turn in his Poe translations, which were being run in the paper.

The hotel was also home to Oscar Wilde for a few weeks in 1883 and to the composer Richard Wagner in the winter of 1861 to 1862.

Musée d'Orsay

1, rue de la Légion d'Honneur (7th arr.)
T: 01 40 49 48 14
Métro: Musée d'Orsay
www.musee-orsay.fr

Édouard Manet was a struggling young artist when he met Baudelaire in 1858 or 1859, but Baudelaire, now considered one of the greatest French art critics of the nineteenth century, saw promise in Manet's talent, and the two became fast friends.

Baudelaire, then working on a translation of Edgar Allan Poe, was living on the third floor of the Hôtel Dieppe (which still stands at 22, rue d'Amsterdam). Just a few blocks away, Manet had his studio at 4, rue Lavoisier, where he painted until 1859, when he left after his fifteen-year-old assistant committed suicide there.

Baudelaire and Manet could often be found at a nearby Flemish tavern at 44, rue de Provence (no longer standing). There, they became infatuated with the ballerina Lola Melea, at whose feet Baudelaire left the following lines:

Among so many beauties that can be
    seen everywhere
I can well understand your wavering
    desire;
But in Lola de Valence one can see
    the glitter
Of the unexpected charm of a pink
    and black gem.

The poem is engraved into the frame of Manet's *Lola de Valence* (1862), which now hangs in the Musée d'Orsay.

The Tuileries

Jardin des Tuileries (1st arr.)
Métro: Tuileries

Baudelaire often accompanied Manet to the Tuileries gardens, where elegant Parisians went to mingle and listen to the biweekly outdoor concerts. These trips were the inspiration for Manet's *La Musique aux Tuileries*, now one of the painter's best-known works. Among the crowd of chic Parisians one finds many of Manet's friends, including the critic Théophile Gautier, the composer Jacques Offenbach, and Baudelaire.

When *La Musique aux Tuileries* was exhibited at the 1863 salon it provoked a scandal: there was no central subject, the figures covered the entire canvas, and some faces were detailed while others were blurred.

Some believe that Baudelaire suggested the idea of *La Musique aux Tuileries* to Manet. Regardless, the contrast between the men's depictions of Paris is striking. For example, Baudelaire's own tribute to the Tuileries and Parisian parks, "Les Veuves," paints parks as "shady sanctuaries where life's cripples come together."

Édouard Manet: *Lola de Valence*, 1862.

Musee d'Orsay, Paris, France. Photo © Erich Lessing / Art Resource, NY.

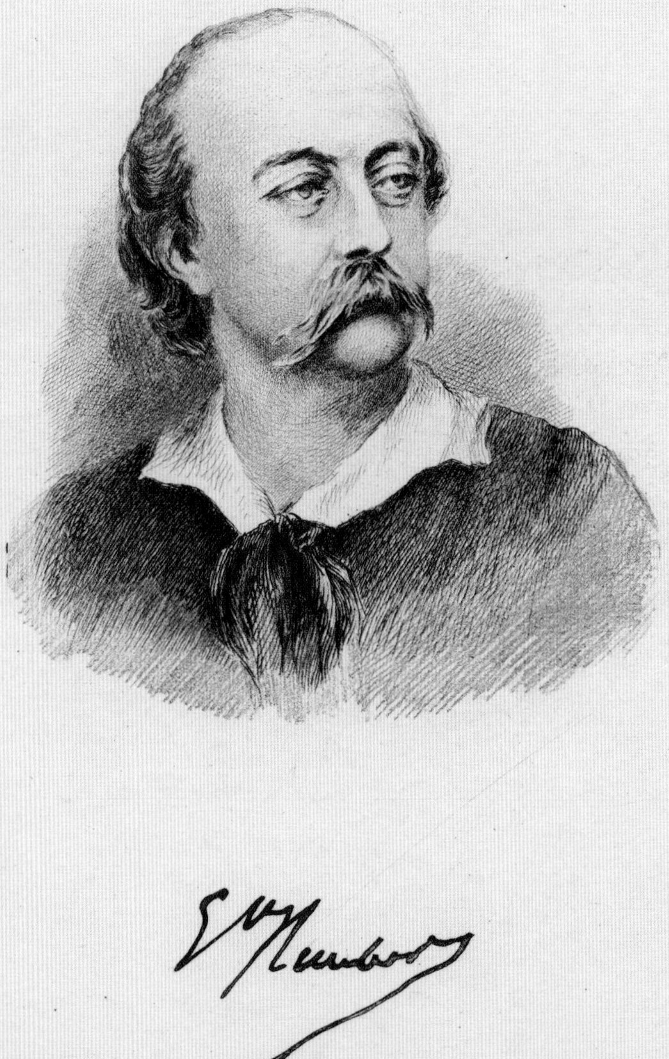

Gustave Flaubert

(1821–1880)

What strikes me as most splendid about Paris is the boulevard. Each time I walk along it, when I get there in the morning, I feel a shock from the asphalt pavement on which every evening so many whores drag their feet.

—Gustave Flaubert
Letter to a friend, c. 1840s

In 1842, Gustave Flaubert wrote to his father about his law studies and his own studiousness. But a letter to a friend suggested a different story.

Twenty-one-year-old Flaubert was living in "superb lodging" on the second floor of 19, rue de l'Est—one of the many streets that would be destroyed in 1855 during the renovation of Paris by Napoleon III's urban planner, Baron Haussmann. By day Flaubert went to school, by night he worked on an autobiographical romance. He hated law and spent most of his time "utterly depressed," later writing:

The walls of my room in the rue de l'Est still remember the terrible curses, the stamping of feet and the cries of distress that poured from me when I was alone. How I roared and how I yawned there.

After failing his law exam in 1843, Flaubert returned home to Rouen, a medieval town in Normandy. Although he made frequent trips to Paris over the next few years, he preferred his parents' home, where he wrote for hours in his room, dressed in a long, white, hooded garment. There he did not need to hide his epilepsy, which was then seen as a suspicious and shameful ailment.

After abandoning two novels, Flaubert began a third, *Madame Bovary*, and moved back to Paris in 1854. He spent the winter at an apartment in the rue de Londres, a new street in the well-to-do *quartier de l'Europe.*

The publication of *Madame Bovary* in 1856 caused an uproar in the capital: the novel, about an adulterous wife, was *too* realistic—Flaubert's critics claimed one could even make out the outline of women's bodies under their clothes. Flaubert was brought to trial at the Palais de Justice, the imposing court that dominates much of the Île de la Cité. He was ultimately acquitted, but not before receiving a warning: literature, he was told, should work to elevate—not echo—the public's morals.

The scandal made Flaubert a public figure. He discarded his white monastic garment and stepped out in polite society in a coat, top hat, and dove gray gloves. He began frequenting literary salons and invited several of his acquaintances to his new apartment along the rue du Temple in the spring of 1861 to hear a reading of his work-in-progress, *Salammbô* (1862).

67

Flaubert's next work, *Sentimental Education* (1869), was based on his two sojourns in Paris—first as a distressed young law student and then as a middle-aged, successful writer who had been seduced by the city's glamour.

When the hero, Frédéric Moreau, first arrives in the capital, he is enthralled by the glistening Seine and the glamorous parade of carriages along the Champs-Élysées, but his vision of the city is transformed during the course of the novel as he becomes increasingly disillusioned with life there. In the novel's early pages, the beauty and promise of Paris is captured in a glimpse of the Tuileries:

> *Behind the Tuileries, the sky turned the colour of the roof-slates. The trees in the gardens faded into two great masses, touched with purple. The gas-lamps were lit; and the waters of the Seine, all grey-green, broke up into silvery rags around its bridges.*

Later in the novel, however, the Tuileries becomes the site of imprisonment for hundreds of starving insurgents.

Sentimental Education covers the years leading up to the Revolution of 1848, which Flaubert himself had witnessed while in Paris. He pored over historic documents and interviewed the revolutionaries of the St.-Antoine quarter, producing a novel that reflected the author's own cynicism toward France's political transformation.

Flaubert looked upon the revolution and Paris with detachment, mocking a city whose history, he thought, was a farce. But Flaubert's detachment and quick condemnation always had to be taken with a grain of salt. His life was a story of craving Paris and fleeing from it; his literature was the same. He wrote,

> *To stop loving Paris is a sign of decadence. Not to be able to live without it is a sign of stupidity.*

Sites

Place de la Concorde

(8th arr.)
Métro: Concorde

Flaubert first met the poet Louise Colet in 1846 at the studio of sculptor James Pradier, an acquaintance from Flaubert's student days in Paris. Flaubert, who was then taking care of his widowed mother in Croisset, Normandy, had made a special trip to see Pradier but upon entering the studio was immediately captivated by the model, who was posing alongside her own half-finished statue. Their turbulent relationship began soon after.

Up until their break in 1854, the couple met sporadically in Paris or between Croisset and the capital. But much of the relationship passed via the post. In her letters, Colet begged her lover to move to Paris. Flaubert often ignored these pleas and instead responded with long monologues on art—a subject that greatly preoccupied him while he was writing *Madame Bovary*.

Pradier's statue of Louise Colet today stands in the place de la Concorde representing the city of Strasbourg.

Former residence of Princess Mathilde

24, rue de Courcelles (8th arr.)
Métro: Miromesnil

The publication of *Salammbô* (1862) turned the spotlight on Flaubert, who was soon summoned to the imperial mansion of the Princess Mathilde Bonaparte at 24, rue de Courcelles. The princess's salon, which was held on Wednesday evenings, was a place of mild liberal dissent—ideal for many of Flaubert's peers, who were able to enjoy the high life without greatly compromising their convictions.

At 9pm on one January evening in 1863, Flaubert, dressed in new trousers, passed the uniformed guard at the entrance and soon discovered that he and his friends were the only ones not wearing diamonds or medals. The evening was a success nonetheless. Napoleon III and Empress Eugénie were in attendance, and the empress asked Flaubert if she could have one of Salammbô's costumes copied as a ballgown (she later abandoned the idea).

Flaubert and the princess shared a particular affection for each other. Flaubert wrote more than 150 letters to her, who by most accounts was plump, imperious, and often weighed down with jewels. But Flaubert, the author who had so mocked the bourgeois in *Madame Bovary*, enjoyed his visits to the princess's home and would gaze at himself in the mirror and comment that he looked like one of the Marquis de Sade's old, evil aristocrats.

Former residence of Flaubert

240, rue du Faubourg St.-Honoré (8th arr.)
Métro: Ternes

Alphonse Daudet, Gustave Flaubert, Edmond de Goncourt, Ivan Turgenev, and Émile Zola called themselves the "hissed authors" because each had been hissed at one point during his career. Sometimes they met in the cafés, other times in Daudet's home at the Hôtel de Lamoignon (which today houses the Bibliothèque historique de la Ville de Paris). But on Sundays they headed to 240, rue du Faubourg St.-Honoré, which was home to Flaubert in the mid-1870s.

Flaubert's latest dwelling was a step down from his previous apartment at 4, rue Murillo, a new, wide, and prosperous street in the 17th arrondissement. Flaubert had moved there shortly after completing *Sentimental Education* in 1869, and his fourth-floor quarters provided a view onto the upscale parc Monceau.

But when his sister's husband faced bankruptcy, Flaubert agreed to trim his expenses in order to save the family. "Three-quarters ruined," he left one of Paris's newest and most prestigious streets for one of its oldest: the rue du Faubourg St.-Honoré, which runs roughly parallel to the Seine for about two kilometers.

At no. 240, Flaubert worked on *Three Tales* (1877) and had Guy de Maupassant over for lunch each week. On Sundays, the hissed authors came to visit. "From three o'clock to six o'clock we went at a gallop through different subjects," wrote Zola.

"When we think of Flaubert, those of us who knew him well in his final years, it is in this white and gold drawing-room that we see him, planting himself in front of us with that characteristic movement of the heels, huge and silent, with his large blue eyes— or else bursting with tremendous paroxysms and shaking his two fists at the ceiling."

Jules Verne

(1828–1905)

Crowds filled the streets; night was beginning to fall, and the luxury shops projected far out onto the sidewalks the brilliant patches of their electric light; streetlamps operated by the Way System—sending a positive electric charge through a thread of mercury— spread an incomparable radiance; they were connected by means of underground wires; at one and the same moment, the hundred thousand streetlamps of Paris came on.

—Jules Verne
Paris in the Twentieth Century, 1863

When Jules Verne wrote *Paris in the Twentieth Century* in 1863, there were no métros, fax machines, or miles of shining streetlamps to be found in the French capital. But these fantastical ideas did exist in the mind of an author who would one day be known for science fiction tales such as *Journey to the Center of the Earth* (1864), *Twenty Thousand Leagues Under the Sea* (1869–1870), and *Around the World in Eighty Days* (1873).

In the early 1860s, Verne was an aspiring writer living with his wife and three children in a series of small apartments in Paris's ninth arrondissement. During the past decade, he had written several plays, magazine articles, and stories, which ranged from pieces about his friend the photographer and balloonist Nadar to the comedy *Mister Chimpanzee* (1860). But his dream to become a writer eluded him, and he received a stack of rejections for his first novel. It was around the time of this failure that Verne is believed to have begun *Paris in the Twentieth Century*.

Verne's Paris of 1960 has five million inhabitants and has spread outward to reach 105 kilometers in diameter. Wide boulevards sweep across Paris: "there are no longer homes, only streets!" In the center, on the Île de la Cité, there are no homes at all, as there is space "only for the Bureau of Commerce, the Palace of Justice, the Prefecture of Police, the cathedral, the morgue—in other words, the means of being declared bankrupt, guilty, jailed, buried, and even rescued."

In this Paris of the future, there are elevators, electronic music, cars, computers, and elevated railways whose trains run on compressed air and electromagnetic force. And although it was hissing gas lamps that dominated Parisian streets in the 1860s, Verne predicted they would one day be supplanted by the hum of electricity—even in Notre Dame, where "the altar shone with electric light, and beams from the same source escaped from the monstrance raised in the priest's hand."

The city's new projects are overseen by the "Minister of Embellishments," a transparent reference to Baron Haussmann, the famed city planner of Verne's day. Among his many projects, Haussmann destroyed swathes of the old city to lay wide boulevards across Paris, joined the suburbs to the city, and raised capital for his projects through France's new national banking system. The city became cleaner and more secure, but a part of Parisians' cultural heritage was destroyed. Paris's streets were straightened at the cost of destroying the city's winding medieval streets and many of its buildings. And while Haussmann managed to improve the city's air and water quality, he did so in part by razing tenement housing and working-class quarters, displacing many of the city's poor.

Likewise, in Verne's novel, Paris's well-lit modernity has come at a price: Latin and Greek are "not only dead, but buried languages," and the Académie Française—the apex of French culture and literature—no longer has any literary members. Banks have replaced old cultural sites, and the city's best men are not poets or philosophers but rather those who speak "in grams and centimeters."

The book's protagonist, sixteen-year-old Michel (named after Verne's son), is a poetry- and Latin-loving misfit through whom Verne vented his own failure as a writer. After quitting his job, Michel spends his days wandering about Paris, spending his few remaining francs on bread made of coal. He winds up in Père-Lachaise, where, stumbling from the tomb of one French writer to the next, he collapses, having starved to death.

Although the novel was Verne's first great step toward the invention of science fiction, he filed it away after his publisher rejected it in 1863. Although the manuscript was not discovered until the end of the twentieth century, the publisher's critiques of the novel were still legible: "If you were a prophet, no one today would ever believe your prophecies."

Sites

La Bourse du Commerce

2, rue de Viarmes (1st arr.)
Métro: Châtelet–Les Halles or Les Halles

> **Michel now stood in front of the Bourse, temple of temples, cathedral of the age; the electric dial showed the time: a quarter to midnight.**

In Jules Verne's vision of the future, the identity of Paris and Parisians is linked to their monetary worth. The Bourse takes on new importance in the Paris of the future, where foreign companies speculate on French properties, and France's own Imperial Real Estate Corporation, "which was gradually seizing all of Paris," owns several French cities.

Verne's vision was based on the extraordinary growth the Bourse experienced during industrialization: in 1800, only seven stocks were quoted on the exchange. By 1853, that number had jumped to 152, and it continued to climb as the canal, railway, and trade industries expanded.

Verne had a personal connection to the Bourse, the "temple of temples, cathedral of the age," whose circular, domed building was erected in the eighteenth century and modified during the nineteenth. While writing *Paris in the Twentieth Century*, Verne awoke each day at 5am to write, then left before 10am to work as a stockbroker for an agency based at 72, rue de Provence in the 9th arrondissement. Verne, whose contempt for money is evident in *Paris in the Twentieth Century*, did not like the work and quit soon after the publication of *Five Weeks in a Balloon* (1863), which was a bestseller and won him a lifetime book contract with his publisher.

Théâtre-Lyrique (Théâtre de la Ville)

2, place du Châtelet (4th arr.)
01 42 74 22 77
www.theatredelaville-paris.com
Métro: Châtelet–Les Halles

Early on in his career, Verne was taken to a party at Victor Hugo's home, where he was introduced to Alexandre Dumas. The popular writer invited him to his castle, the Monte Cristo, where Verne was stunned by the turbaned servants, high towers, and waterfalls. Dumas took an immediate liking to Verne and shared his theater box with him, where the two watched Dumas' *The Three Musketeers*. He also encour-

aged the unknown writer to incorporate more scientific elements into his stories, and even staged one of Verne's early plays, *Broken Straws*, at his theater, the Théâtre-Historique (soon to be renamed the Théâtre-Lyrique, and today known as the Théâtre de la Ville).

Verne would be hired by this same theater in 1852 to work as a secretary. On the side, he tried his hand at operettas, but to little success. He left the theater in 1856 to begin a more lucrative, but much hated, job as a stockbroker.

Situated on the place du Châtelet and overlooking the Seine, today's Théâtre de la Ville is mainly faithful to the theater's original nineteenth-century design (the first building was consumed by fire in 1871).

Mark Twain

(1835–1910)

The gentle reader will never, never know
what a consummate ass he can become,
until he goes abroad.

—Mark Twain
The Innocents Abroad, 1869

French School, (19th century): General view of the
Exposition Universelle in 1867, taken from the
Trocadero hill, Paris, 1867.

Musee de la Ville de Paris, Musee Carnavalet, Paris, France, Archives
Charmet / Bridgeman Art Library.

"Everything is charming to the eye," wrote Mark Twain, recalling his arrival in Paris in 1867. Famous landmarks rolled past him as though in a dream—everything was foreign and yet already familiar.

> *It was like meeting an old friend when we read "Rue de Rivoli" on the street corner; we knew the genuine vast palace of the Louvre as well as we knew its picture.*

The celebrated American author (born Samuel Langhorne Clemens) who would later write *Tom Sawyer* (1876) and *Huckleberry Finn* (1884) was in his early thirties when he found himself in the "beautiful dream" that he called Paris. He had been sent by American newspapers to write about his trip through Europe. In the French capital for only five days, he was to report on the Universal Exposition—the pride of Napoleon III and the prefect of Paris, Baron Haussmann, who had transformed the capital and razed its crooked, narrow alleyways and replaced them with wide, gleaming boulevards.

> *I basked in the happiness of being for once in my life drifting with the tide of a great popular movement. Everybody was going to Europe—I was going to Europe. Everybody was going to the famous Paris Exposition—I, too, was going to the Paris Exposition.*

In fact, Twain spent barely two hours at the exposition. Cyrus McCormick's reaper was on display, as was Elias Howe's sewing machine, but Twain was far more interested in people watching than inventions, and he left the expo upon hearing that Napoleon III and the sultan of Turkey were to review 25,000 troops from the Arc de Triomphe. Twain hoped to catch a glimpse of the emperor, "the representative of the highest modern civilization, progress, and refinement."

Twain admired Napoleon III and described to American readers the work the emperor had undertaken in his city. "He condemns a whole street at a time, assesses the damages, pays them, and rebuilds superbly." This was no clearer than in the working-class neighborhood of the Faubourg St.-Antoine—historically the heart of revolutionary foment, and invoked in Victor Hugo's *Les Misérables*. As Twain observed, Napoleon III was well aware of the advantage narrow streets posed for creating barricades:

Here the people who begin the revolutions . . . take as much genuine pleasure in building a barricade as they do in cutting a throat or shoving a friend into the Seine. . . . But they will build no more barricades; they will break no more soldiers' heads with paving stones. Louis Napoleon has taken care of all that.

Twain set out to take in the other sites of the city, which he dutifully recorded in his book *The Innocents Abroad*. After a visit to the "brown old Gothic pile" of Notre Dame, he was enchanted by the "limitless park" of the Bois de Boulogne. Twain found everything so "fearfully and wonderfully Frenchy," like the cancan, the new dance sweeping the French stage: "Twenty sets formed, the music struck up, and then—I placed my hands before my face for very shame," wrote Twain. "But I looked through my fingers."

The point of the cancan, Twain explained, was to "dance as wildly, as noisily, as furiously as you can; expose yourself as much as possible if you are a woman; and kick as high as you can,

Mark Twain, c. 1870s.
© Corbis.

no matter which sex you belong to. . . . I suppose French morality is not of that straight-laced description which is shocked at trifles." (He would be less kind a decade later, when, after summering in France, he declared that the country had "neither winter nor summer nor morals.")

But Twain was not charmed by all things Parisian. He was unimpressed by the Louvre, which he believed held too many paintings dedicated to the "nauseous adulation of princely patrons." Nor did he appreciate the independent and sexually assertive young bohemian women of the Latin Quarter, whom he found neither coquettish nor attractive, and in fact rather like "all Frenchwomen I ever saw—homely." He longed for soap and believed that he and his friends could find the country's famed wines exciting only "if we had chosen to drink a sufficiency of them."

Although Twain's own French was poor, he was dismayed to discover that the French did not "speaky ze Angleesh parfaitemaw," and he was perplexed that bartenders could not understand his drink orders of a whiskey straight, let alone a Santa Cruz Punch or an Eye-Opener.

The Innocents Abroad, which poked fun at both European and American manners, was a great success when published in 1868. "The idea of a steamer-load of Americans going on a prolonged picnic to Europe and the Holy Land is itself almost sufficiently delightful," read one review in the *Atlantic Monthly*. But the book's appeal went beyond poking fun at Americans abroad. Twain's book pitted a bunch of bumbling, but often well-meaning Americans against the bizarre customs, foods, and thinking of foreign cultures. The Civil War had ended only a few years before, and the US was still divided by deep-seated political and cultural differences, but Twain's "innocents" abroad were not Northerners or Southerners but quite simply, Americans.

Twain's financial success with *The Innocents Abroad* and his following books allowed him to return to live in Europe for nine years near the end of the nineteenth century. This time, however, he was less enamored by France and seemed particularly disturbed by its morals and weather. In an 1879 speech, he listed the "objects of which Paris folks are fond—litera-

ture, art, medicine and adultery." And the following year he wrote to a friend:

> . . . *anywhere is better than Paris. Paris the cold, Paris the drizzly, Paris the rainy, Paris the damnable. Let us change the proverb; Let us say all bad Americans go to Paris when they die. No, let us not say it for this adds a new horror to Immortality.*

But Twain still reserved some fondness for the French. After returning to the US in 1900, he occasionally practiced his French in his living room in front of his cats. Despite his thick Missouri accent, he claimed his cats clapped frantically whenever he gave impassioned speeches in that language. As for the French, however, "in Paris they simply stared when I spoke to them in French; I never did succeed in making those idiots understand their language."

Sites

Twain's former residence

169, rue de l'Université (7th arr.)
Métro: Pont de l'Alma

Twain returned to Europe with his family in 1891, living in various European countries during his nine years abroad. In 1895, the family was living in a "charming mansion" at 169, rue de l'Université, where Twain's wife, Livy, was fond of hosting dinner parties. Twain wrote,

> In that pleasant Paris house [Livy] gathered little dinner companions together once or twice a week, and it goes without saying that in these circumstances my defects had a large chance for display.

Grand Hôtel du Louvre

Place André Malraux (1st arr.)
T: 01 44 58 38 38
www.hoteldulouvre.com
Métro: Palais-Royal

"To close our first day in Paris cheerfully and pleasantly, we now sought our grand room in the Grand Hôtel du Louvre and climbed into our sumptuous bed to read and smoke. . . ." Unfortunately, Paris's new gas lamps burned brightly along the boulevards, but there were none to be found in France's first luxury hotel, and Twain was unable to read as planned.

The next day, the hotel set Twain up with three guides who offered to take him around the city. The first looked like a pirate; the second spoke abominable English. But the third "stepped as gently and as daintily as a cat crossing a muddy street," and seemed the very definition of the French gentleman. Twain was thrilled to make his acquaintance—until he handed over his hotel business card and they discovered that his name was the decidedly un-French "Billfinger."

Although Twain had been hoping for a Henri de Montmorency or Armand de la Chartreuse to lead him about Paris, he settled on Billfinger, who was a most polite and respectful guide until Twain made the gregarious American gesture of demanding that Billfinger eat at the same table as his clients.

From then on, Twain and his party found themselves taken to more restaurants and cafés than sites. Billfinger also insisted on taking Twain to every silk shop in town, in the hopes of getting a commission from the shopkeepers.

Twain published his Billfinger tale in *The Innocents Abroad*, where he warned his hungry guide: "I shall visit Paris again someday, and then let the guides beware! I shall go in my war paint—I shall carry my tomahawk along."

The hotel, whose construction was ordered by Napoleon III in 1855, moved in 1887 to the other side of the place du Palais-Royal, where it stands today. The hotel's most famous inhabitant was French impressionist Camille Pissaro, who painted *La place du Théâtre Français*, *La rue St.-Honoré*, and *L'avenue de l'Opéra* while living there.

Mark Twain: Map of Paris from *The Galaxy*, November 1870.

Cornell University Library, Making of America Digital Collection.

MARK TWAIN'S MAP OF PARIS.

Émile Zola
(1840–1902)

Then, as he turned towards the city, all Paris spread itself out at his feet, a limpid, lightsome Paris, beneath the pink glow of that spring-like evening. The endless billows of house-roofs showed forth with wonderful distinctness, and one could have counted the chimney stacks and the little black streaks of the windows by the million.

—Émile Zola,
Paris, Three Cities Trilogy, 1894–1898

It was the winter of 1861 and Émile Zola was short of food and forced to dine on the few sparrows he could catch on his windowsill at 11, rue Soufflot. Shivering in his threadbare coat, the young writer from Aix gazed out onto the rooftops of Paris and envisioned a novel in which "Paris, with its ocean of roofs, would be a character, something like a Greek chorus."

His first novel, *Claude's Confession*, was published a few years later in 1865. It shocked the public with its realistic descriptions of poverty and sex, and got Zola fired from his advertising job. Penniless, Zola embarked on a career in journalism. In his provocative reviews he attacked the "capes and swords" literature of the Romantics and favored the author "who makes an attempt to introduce the brutal and implacable truth, the drama of life with all its developments and audacities." He argued for literature that would honestly depict the modern industrialized world, not run away from it. For Zola, this meant depicting contemporary Paris, from its unsanitary sewage system and the living conditions of the city's poor to descriptions of prostitutes and the lives of courtesans. Although the public was first repelled

by these details, they warmed to Zola's stark portrait of Paris in *The Dram Shop* (1876), which the author called "the first novel about the people which has the true scent of the people."

> *The Seine carried greasy mats, with old corks and vegetable peelings, a pile of garbage that lingered for a moment in an eddy in the sinister depths of the water, darkened by the shadow of the arch; while, from the bridge itself they could hear the passing cabs and omnibuses, the rumble of Paris, though all they could see of the city were its roofs, to right and left, as though from the bottom.*

Although Zola's own poverty paled in comparison with that of his working-class characters, money was a constant worry during his early years. At one point he sold wool from his mattress, another time he was forced to borrow six hundred francs from his friend the painter Édouard Manet.

But with the success of *The Dram Shop*, Zola's situation improved. The lifestyle of the straightlaced author changed little, although he began to indulge in higher-quality food, and Guy de Maupassant accused him of eating three times the amount of their other friends. Zola also entered the world of theater, with an adaptation of *The Dram Shop* making its stage debut on January 1879. Although occasional cries of "Death to the naturalist!" were heard opening night at the Ambigu Theater, critics were virtually unanimous in their praise. To celebrate the play's success, a ball was held at the Élysée Montmartre Theater (which still stands at 72, boulevard de Rochechouart in the 18th arrondissement). More than 1,500 guests were in attendance, with the men dressed as laborers and the ladies as laundresses.

By that time, Zola was firmly fixed as a leader of the naturalist movement, which preferred exhaustive, realistic detail to fanciful plots and flowery language. Each Thursday, he and his wife, Alexandrine, hosted a salon largely made up of younger naturalist writers, including Paul Alexis and Guy de Maupassant. Zola was also close to older, more successful writers, meeting with Alphonse Daudet, Gustave Flaubert, Edmond de Goncourt, and Ivan Turgenev. The group of five called themselves "the hissed authors," having all been booed at one point in their literary careers.

They often met at the Café Riche (then at 16, boulevard des Italiens) and their long, raucous evenings could last until two or three in the morning. Café Riche appeared in several of Zola's novels as a window onto Paris's bustling parade of people and sights:

> Directly below the window, the tables of the Café Riche basked in the glare of its lamps, whose light reached to the middle of the roadway. . . . The parade was endless, moreover, renewing itself with tiresome regularity; it was a strangely-mixed crowd, yet always the same, surrounded by bright colors and punctuated by dark voids in the fantastic chaos of a thousand dancing flames, pouring from the shops, coloring the storefronts and kiosks.

As Zola's fame grew, he became a frequent target of conservatives outraged by his true-to-life, "immoral" writings. Women wrote to proposition him, priests to scold him. Others accused him of writing about subjects that were foreign to him—little did they know that Zola's research for *Nana* (1880), his novel about Parisian courtesans, was based in part on consultations with his friends Maupassant and Flaubert (both of whom were plagued by syphilis).

According to Flaubert, Zola was "a colossus with dirty feet, nevertheless a colossus"—a comment that referred just as much to Zola's importance to French literature as to his 5'7", 210-pound frame. But by the time he was fifty, a new Zola had emerged: the serious family man had shed fifty pounds and was having an affair with a younger woman. He purchased a new, luxurious apartment at 21, *bis* rue de Bruxelles (today marked by a plaque), close to his mistress's home.

But the relative financial and social stability Zola enjoyed as a successful author was disrupted in 1894, when a Jewish army captain, Alfred Dreyfus, was convicted on trumped-up charges that he was a spy for the German army. Anti-Semitism had risen noticeably during the Third Republic, and Dreyfus was an easy scapegoat. When a military lieutenant discovered that the notes used to convict Dreyfus were forgeries, he attempted to reopen the case—and was promptly transferred to Tunisia.

The case would likely have faded away had Zola not published "*J'accuse*!" a scathing denunciation of the cover-up. Zola was found guilty of libeling the army, and the author slipped off to England to avoid imprisonment. He did not return until the summer of 1899, when the appeals court annulled the court decision.

But the Dreyfus affair was not forgotten. A few years later, Zola and Alexandrine were returning to their apartment on the rue de Bruxelles after having summered in Médan. They arrived home September 28, 1902, and lit a coal fire in their bedroom to combat the fall chill. That night Zola awoke, stumbled out of his bed, and fell to the floor. The next morning, the servants, receiving no answer when they knocked, had the couple's door broken down. Alexandrine was alive but unconscious; Zola was found lifeless on the floor. An investigation revealed that their chimney had been blocked shortly before their return to Paris—the work, some believed, of assassins.

Although he was initially laid to rest at the Montmartre cemetery, Zola would eventually be transported to the Panthéon. In the ten novels he set in Paris, he managed to describe the city as he had first encountered it as a poor, aspiring writer from the provinces. His novels were filled with "the immensity of Paris," a "vast grayness tinted blue at the edges, with deep valleys in which roofs swelled and rolled like the sea."

Sites

Les Halles

(1st arr.)

Métro: Châtelet–Les Halles

> All around him the sun seemed to set the vegetables afire. . . . The plump hearts of the lettuces were ablaze, the row of greens burst into wonderful life, the carrots bled, the turnips became incandescent, in this triumph of fire.
> —*The Belly of Paris*, 1873

Although Zola enjoyed good health throughout his life, he suffered long bouts of insomnia. During one of his sleepless nights, he decided to rise and leave his apartment, eventually making his way to Les Halles. It was his first visit to Paris's central market —a chaotic mix of colors and smells— and his bad eyesight led him to mistake stalls of violets for piles of beef.

It was this initial experience, and subsequent visits, that would inspire Zola's 1873 work *The Belly of Paris*.

Since the twelfth century, merchants had gathered each morning at the market, which was Paris's most important source for foodstuffs. "Les Halles is the Louvre of the people!" declared Napoleon III, who undertook its modernization by erecting new pavilions of iron and glass to improve food distribution. Its multiacre, roofed market, wrote Zola, consisted of

> . . . enormous, symmetrically built palaces, light and airy as crystal, whose fronts sparkled with countless streaks of light filtering through endless Venetian shutters. Gleaming between the slender pillar shafts these narrow golden bars seemed like ladders of light mounting to the gloomy line of the lower roofs, and then soaring aloft till they reached the jumble of higher ones, thus describing the open framework of immense square halls, where in the yellow flare of the gas lights a multitude of vague, grey, slumbering things was gathered together.

Zola aimed to create a vivid catalog of the labyrinthine market—the vegetables covering the sidewalks of the rue Turbigo, the impenetrable path blocking the rue Pierre-Lescot, and the carts forming a blockade at the rue Rambuteau and boulevard Sébastopol. But the book was also a denunciation of Second Empire decadence and corruption of a place where the wealthy grow fatter as the poor are left behind.

Today's Les Halles is a far cry from the Les Halles of Zola's time. The colorful market was torn down in the 1970s in order to install a park and underground shopping mall. The city has recently undertaken a long-term study to envision a new Les Halles.

Opéra-Comique
Place Boieldieu (2nd arr.)
T: 01 42 44 45 40
www.opera-comique.com
Métro: Richelieu-Drouot

> My dear Bruneau, I have nothing to do tomorrow and I shall no doubt go to the Opéra-Comique; it is simply the case of a man's curiosity. . . . I'll find a quiet spot in the rear, so as not to disturb you.
> —Letter to Alfred Bruneau, June 1891

Opera was a new passion for Zola, who had previously criticized the genre for its unrealistic characters. This changed, however, when he met the composer Alfred Bruneau in 1888. It was a period in which Zola feared his literary career had stagnated, and the opportunity to collaborate with a young and talented musician such as Bruneau tempted the forty-eight-year-old author.

Zola's note to Bruneau was written just days before the June 18, 1891, opening of Zola and Bruneau's *The Dream* at the Opéra-Comique. In addition to *The Dream*, three other Zola-Bruneau collaborations were performed at this theater: *The Attack on the Mill*, *Hurricane*, and *The Child King*.

The Opéra-Comique was founded in 1714 as an alternative to traditional opera, which did not allow for spoken words. Although the theater offered a more casual approach to the genre, it did not lack in elegance. The façade was often compared to that of an Italian palace, and in Zola's day each loge included a small bell so that opera-goers could ring for a waiter. The current interior dates to 1898 and welcomes visitors with elegant marble and mosaic floors and three tiers of golden balconies.

Chalet des Îles

Lac Inférieur du Bois de Boulogne
(16th arr.)
T: 01–42–88–84–09
www.lechaletdesiles.net
Métro: Porte Dauphine

With the June 1893 publication of
Doctor Pascal, Balzac's twenty-three-
year, twenty-volume *Rougon-Macquart*
series came to an end. In honor of
the occasion, a celebration was held
June 21 at the idyllic Chalet des Îles,
located on an island in a lake of the
Bois de Boulogne park. The chalet,
which was transported from Switzerland and reconstructed on the island
as a gift from Napoleon III to his wife,
Eugénie, had become a popular spot
for Paris's literary crowd and a logical
—if lavish—choice for a party in
Zola's honor.

Today, the Chalet des Îles is the
restaurant of choice for park-goers and
couples looking for a quiet, romantic
meal. In order to reach the island,
guests take a one-minute ferry ride
across the lake. There they are greeted
by the restaurant's staff or, sometimes, one of the many peacocks and
ducks roaming the small island. The
restaurant serves traditional French
food at moderate prices.

Basilique du Sacré-Coeur de Montmartre

Place du Parvis du Sacré-Coeur
(18th arr.)
www.sacre-coeur-montmartre.fr
Métro: Anvers

> And as they turned they perceived
> the basilica of the Sacred Heart, still
> domeless but already looking huge
> indeed in the moonbeams, whose
> clear white light accentuated its out-
> lines and brought them into sharp
> relief against a mass of shadows.
> Under the pale nocturnal sky, the edi-
> fice showed like a colossal monster,
> symbolical of provocation and sover-
> eign dominion.
> —*Paris, Three Cities Trilogy*,
> 1894–1898

Zola was critical of Sacré-Cœur (Sacred
Heart), whose slow rise from the top
of Montmartre began in 1875. Undertaken by the National Assembly as
expiation for France's troubled post-
revolutionary times, its first stones
were laid in 1875 and it was still unfinished when Zola wrote *Paris* (1896),
whose character Pierre, a former
priest, contemplates destroying it:

> One cannot imagine anything more
> preposterous than Paris, our great
> Paris, crowned and dominated by this
> temple raised to the glorification of
> the absurd. Is it not outrageous that
> common sense should receive such
> a smack after so many centuries of
> science, that Rome should claim the
> right of triumphing in this insolent
> fashion, on our loftiest height in the
> full sunlight?

With wide public and governmental support, little notice was taken of Zola's
protest. The Romano-Byzantine style
basilica was fully completed in 1914,
and today is one of Paris's most popular tourist attractions. The interior of
the church boasts one of the world's
largest mosaics. Sunday mass is held
at 11am, 6pm, and 10:15pm.

Paul Verlaine
(1844–1896)

Arthur Rimbaud
(1854–1891)

The moon, that lucent luminary,

Lit up the bridges sinister;

Billows lapped Paris, cleansing her—

Paris, gay as a cemetery.

—Paul Verlaine
"Dream," *Invectives*, 1896

Henri Fantin-Latour: *Coin de Table*, 1872. From left to right: (members of *Les Vilains bonhommes*) Paul Verlaine, Arthur Rimbaud, Elzear Bonnier, Leon Valade, Emile Blemont, Jean Aicart, Ernest d'Hervilly, Camille Pelletan.

Musée d'Orsay, Paris, France. Photo © Erich Lessing/Art Resource, NY.

The raggedy seventeen-year-old who arrived in Paris on September 24, 1871, was not the schoolboy Paul Verlaine and his literary friends had expected. They had invited the young provincial to the capital after Verlaine had received some of his verses in the mail. The group, whose nickname—the *Vilains bonhommes* (Nasty Fellows)—belied their rather tame poetry and lives, were in awe of young Arthur Rimbaud's "lines of terrifying beauty."

"Terrifying" was the word many of the *Vilains bonhommes* would again use after coming face-to-face with Rimbaud. Enchanted by his poems, they made a space for him at their dinners and took him into their homes—which he promptly wrecked. At the first meeting, held near St.-Sulpice, Rimbaud shocked the artists and poets by declaring the end of the alexandrine—the classical meter that had ruled French poetry since the days of Jean Racine. At another gathering, he inserted the word *merde* after every line of poetry read by one member, then he stabbed another artist.

Rimbaud was indeed a terror: he blew smoke up horses' noses, rarely bathed, and flicked the lice in his hair at priests passing by. He was an anarchist who declared that the Louvre and the Bibliothèque Nationale should be burned to the ground. The only person who seemed charmed by his behavior was Verlaine, who, despite being newly married with a wife and child, was attracted to the younger poet.

The two men were soon inseparable. Verlaine took Rimbaud to Café du Gaz, Le Rat Mort, and Café Cluny, where Rimbaud left behind a few scribbled lines of scatological verse. They also frequented the cafés along the rue de Rivoli, where, as Verlaine later recalled, under "the screaming gas lamps," the twenty-seven-year-old grew increasingly infatuated with Rimbaud. Soon, he began to dress like the young man, and his wife complained that he was spending all of his time and money on Rimbaud, going so far as to abandon normal, bourgeois attire for "horrible scarves and floppy hats."

Both poets were more concerned with imagination and the beauty of verse than they were with Paris's ills, morals, or modernity. Unlike the Romantics before them, for whom Paris—and its transformation—had been a central theme, the city was simply one of many settings for Verlaine

Arthur Rimbaud, 1870.
Library of Congress Prints and Photographs Division, Washington, D.C.

and Rimbaud. Verlaine's Paris, when it did appear in his poems, was often little more than a quiet backdrop, though in one poem he describes *"le long ennui de vos haussmanneries"*—a pejorative reference to the geometric city blocks created by Baron Haussmann.

An identifiable Parisian cityscape was even more rare in Rimbaud, whose poems were often collages of the cities he had seen. However, in an early poem written in 1871, he speaks concretely of Paris, "radiant blue-starred, one evening, by the red flashes of bombs!" The poem, "Paris se repeuple," is full of "dead palaces" hidden under "planks"—possibly a reference to destitute and bombed-out Paris in the days following its siege by the Prussians in 1870.

Although homosexuality was still taboo in French society, many of the *Vilains bonhommes* had previously overlooked Verlaine's discreet preference for men. But their attitude changed with the presence of Rimbaud, whose more overt homosexuality they found shocking. One day, Verlaine and Rimbaud met at the Odéon—one of the more bohemian theaters at the time—and the two men strolled

through the foyer while in an embrace. A gossip column soon revealed having spotted "Paul Verlaine arm-in-arm with a charming young lady, Mlle Rimbaut [*sic*]."

Verlaine became increasingly estranged from his friends and family, and finally, in the summer of 1872, Rimbaud convinced Verlaine to leave his sick wife and head with him to Belgium. The next year was spent in Belgium and England, in hotel rooms and small flats, where the two lovers were alternately a loving and a bickering, violent couple.

Verlaine was twenty-nine, and Rimbaud nearly nineteen, when their relationship came to an end. In July 1873, they were in Belgium, arguing about Rimbaud's planned return to Paris, when Verlaine pulled out a gun and shot Rimbaud just above his wrist. Later, they were walking back from the hospital when Verlaine reached for his gun a second time. Rimbaud ran to the nearest policeman, and Verlaine was sentenced to two years in jail.

Soon after, Rimbaud abandoned poetry. He traveled to thirteen different countries and, among his many jobs, was a construction worker in Cyprus and a gunrunner for Menelik II of Abyssinia, before dying of cancer at age thirty-seven. The four small works he left behind established him as a poetic visionary and early modernist. He became immortalized as France's favorite antihero, "the poet of revolt, and the greatest of them all," as Albert Camus wrote.

After a prison sentence, a ten-year exile, another lover, and a divorce, Verlaine returned to Paris in 1882 to discover he was no longer welcome among his old friends. He spent his days in the cafés, spending the little money he had on absinthe. His prose had taken on an increasingly wistful, nostalgic tone, in which Paris seemed "sad and gay, crazy and wise."

By the mid-1880s, however, Verlaine's friends were coming around. Time had made a legend of Verlaine—a talented poet ruined by a romantic obsession with a wild youth. He was also publishing again: the Chat Noir, the lively cabaret then at 12, rue Victor-Massé, was publishing a weekly review and included many of Verlaine's new poems. He wrote prefaces for two of Rimbaud's works, saw his own poetry rereleased, and published new works, including *Love* (1888) and *Parallelism* (1889). In 1894

the review *La Plume* elected Verlaine its Prince of Poets.

Verlaine died at the age of fifty-two in 1896. He spent his final years in poverty, moving from one slum to the next, and drinking at Le Procope or Le Café François 1er, then at 73, rue Soufflot.

In 1911, fifteen years after Verlaine's death, the government rasied a monument in his honor in the Luxembourg Gardens. Oscar Wilde joked that it should have been placed in François 1er, as "the hero's statue must be on his life's battlefield."

Paul Verlaine, 1891.

Sites

Verlaine's former residence

14, rue Nicolet (18th arr.)
Métro: Château Rouge

As the train carrying seventeen-year-old Arthur Rimbaud rolled into the Gare de l'Est, Paul Verlaine instead arrived at the Gare du Nord. His excitement about the young poet's arrival had warranted a few celebratory drinks, and he had forgotten at which station Rimbaud's train was set to arrive.

With no one there to greet him, Rimbaud set out for Verlaine's home in Montmartre. As he traveled north through the city, artists' homes gave way to windmills and vineyards. Finally he reached the rue Nicolet, a small street inhabited by respectable bourgeois families who were suspicious of poets and bohemians.

With shaggy hair and a shredded tie, Rimbaud looked more like a peasant than a poet. His blue, cotton-knit socks, and his strong provincial accent came as a shock to Verlaine's wife and in-laws, who had been looking forward to meeting the man Verlaine had touted as France's next great poet. Soon after Rimbaud's arrival, objects went missing, and Verlaine's wife,

Mathilde, had to tell Rimbaud that it was improper to sunbathe in front of the house. The boy stayed out late drinking with Verlaine and coerced him into spending a great deal of money.

Soon, Mathilde had had enough, and Rimbaud was sent off to another unsuspecting host.

Former residences of the *Vilains bonhommes*

10, rue de Buci (6th arr.)
Métro: Mabillon
13, rue Séguier (7th arr.)
Métro: St.-André-des-Arts or St.-Michel

When Rimbaud was kicked out of the Verlaines' home in Montmartre, members of the *Vilains bonhommes* came to the rescue. Théodore de Banville, the leader of the Parnassian poets, offered a maid's room at 10, rue de Buci and pooled a bit of money in order to provide Rimbaud with a daily allowance of three francs.

On the autumn evening in which Rimbaud was to move in, a loud cry interrupted the dinner of the rue de Buci's bourgeois residents. Banville rushed outside to see what the matter was, and spotted Rimbaud in a tree, tearing off his clothes and tossing

them onto the roof. Soon, he was wearing little more than what Banville described as "mythological" costume. Rimbaud explained, "I couldn't possibly occupy such a clean and virginal room with my old, lice-ridden rags." Although it may have been an excuse, Rimbaud did suffer from a bad case of lice, and even wrote a poem on the subject, "Les Chercheuses de poux."

Rimbaud did not last long at Banville's apartment, since he soon took to going to bed with his clothes on, muddying his sheets, smashing the porcelain in the room, and selling the furniture. A week after moving in, he was asked to leave. Verlaine found him new quarters with his friend Charles Cros, who was living nearby at 13, rue Séguier. Cros was a poet and inventor who was considered an eccentric by the other Parnassians. In 1869, he had published a strategy for communicating with inhabitants of Mars and Venus, and when Rimbaud arrived he was trying to make precious stones in his apartment.

On the first morning of their cohabitation, Rimbaud was annoyed to find his boots freshly polished. He tromped on them outside, then spat tobacco on them. Later, at Le Rat Mort café in the place Pigalle, Rimbaud put sulfuric acid in Cros' drink when the latter left the table. In the coming days, Rimbaud also managed to destroy one of Cros' plaster busts and used the review in which his poems were published as toilet paper. Somehow, though, he managed to charm Cros, who never asked him to leave. Nevertheless, Rimbaud disappeared after two weeks without saying goodbye.

Hôtel Cluny Sorbonne

8, rue Victor Cousin (5th arr.)
T: 01 43 54 66 66
www.hotel-cluny.fr
Métro: Luxembourg

Although at Verlaine's request he had agreed to leave Paris for a while, Rimbaud returned to Paris on May 25, 1872. There was no question of him staying with Verlaine—he was the very reason Verlaine was on bad terms with his wife. For the next forty-four days, Rimbaud moved from one hotel to the next, preferring to sleep on the roof whenever possible. Early each day, he could be found at his favorite bar on the rue St.-Jacques—the Académie d'Absinthe, so named because instead of forty academicians it boasted forty barrels of absinthe.

One of Rimbaud's homes in May was at 22, rue Monsieur-le-Prince, which looked onto a garden in the picturesque Lycée St.-Louis:

> There were enormous trees beneath my narrow window. At three in the morning, the candlelight grows dim and all the birds start singing at once in the trees. It's over. No more work. I had to gaze at the trees and the sky, transfixed by that inexpressible first hour of morning. I could see the school dormitories, completely silent. And already I could hear the delicious, resonant, clattering sounds of the carts on the boulevards.
>
> I smoked my hammerhead pipe and spat on the roof-tiles—because my room was a garret. At five o'clock, I'd go down to buy some bread. It was that time of day. Workers are up and about all over the place. Time to get drunk at the wine-shop—time for me, that is. I'd go back to eat and then get into bed at seven in the morning, when the sun brings the woodlice out from under the roof-tiles.

Near the rue Monsieur-le-Prince stands another Rimbaud address from that period, the Hôtel de Cluny. Although the hotel is now a respectable tourist dwelling, in Rimbaud's time it drew boarders who didn't mind its "three-square-meter" rooms. Nevertheless, Rimbaud was struck by the prettiness of his room (no. 62), as well as its view onto "a bottomless courtyard."

But soon the charm of rooftop sleeping wore thin: "I drink water all night long, I don't see the dawn, I don't sleep, and I'm stifling," he wrote. On July 7, he found Verlaine and convinced him to go to Belgium.

Oscar Wilde

(1854–1900)

The moon is like a yellow seal
Upon a dark blue envelope
And down below the dusky slope
Like a black sword of polished steel
With flickering damascenes of gold
Flows the dark Seine.

—Oscar Wilde
from his notebooks, 1884

Napoleon Sarony: Oscar Wilde, c. 1882.
Library of Congress Prints and Photographs Division, Washington, D.C.

Oscar Wilde left England in January 1883, convinced that there was "no modern literature outside France" and that Paris was the place to be. Ready to assume his place among his literary idols, he chose the Hôtel Voltaire—the same hotel in which Charles Baudelaire had stayed. While writing in his room, Wilde wore a white wool dressing gown similar to the monk's cowl once worn by Honoré de Balzac, and when he went out, he carried an ivory and turquoise cane much like the one Balzac had owned. His affinity for Paris and its writers was embodied in the lines he would write a decade later in *The Picture of Dorian Gray* (1891):

> *The hero [of the book], the wonderful young Parisian in whom the romantic and the scientific temperaments were so strangely blended, became to him a kind of prefiguring type of himself. And, indeed, the whole book seemed to him to contain the story of his own life, written before he had lived it.*

Wilde soon made the rounds of Paris's literary and artistic community, taking flowers to Sarah Bernhardt; watching an aging Victor Hugo fall asleep at his own party; and encountering the disgraced poet Paul Verlaine.

Parental pressure and questions about Wilde's sexuality prompted the writer to return to England in the spring of 1883 in order to marry. Although he honeymooned in Paris, his next long-term stay would not come until 1891 at the age of thirty-seven. By then he was famous. His novel, *The Portrait of Dorian Gray*, had both scandalized and enthralled English society and was enthusiastically received by Wilde's literary friends across the Channel.

Wilde's winter in Paris was so filled with social engagements that *L'Écho de Paris* declared him *le great event* of the Parisian literary salons. But Wilde still managed to shock: upon arriving at Marcel Proust's home for dinner, Wilde took great offense at the tacky décor and left before the aperitif.

Wilde was busy that winter with *Salomé* (1892), a play inspired by a biblical tale, which he had decided to write in French. He declared the play would see him nominated to the Académie Française. Instead, it was banned in England for its illegal depiction of a biblical scene; Wilde in turn threatened to renounce his English citizenship and become French.

But Wilde, now thirty-eight, was soon consumed by other passions. Although married, he had recently become involved with a wealthy poet, Lord Alfred Douglas, and was making increased references to homosexuality in his works during a time in which the practice was considered a crime in England. His friends in both England and France were worried: "So much taste," warned his friend Edgar Degas, "may lead to prison."

The painter's words proved prophetic. In 1895, having provoked the wrath of his lover's powerful father, Wilde was thrown into an English prison for sodomy and sentenced to two years of prison and hard labor. He emerged a broken man.

After completing his prison sentence, Wilde made his way back to Paris with little money to his name. But he soon found that "those Parisians who licked my conqueror's boots only ten years before" now pretended not to recognize him. Poor and disgraced, Wilde lingered in the cafés along the boulevard St.-Germain. One time, a friend caught him sitting at a café in the rain, unable to leave because he had no money to pay his bill.

The sympathetic proprietor of the Hôtel d'Alsace (now called L'Hôtel) took a liking to Wilde and allowed him to take one of the rooms at 13, rue des Beaux-Arts. He provided Wilde with breakfast and lunch, and several bottles of Courvoisier each week.

By his early forties, Wilde was suffering from various ailments, and by late September of 1900, he was bedridden at the Hôtel d'Alsace—the result of the syphilis he had caught in his youth from a prostitute. He drank absinthe to make the hours pass and, when his morphine began to wear off, took to champagne. "My wallpaper and I," he said, "are fighting a duel to the death. One or the other of us has to go."

One morning near the end of his life, he was riding on one of the *bateaux-mouches* in the Seine when his path crossed with that of a countess he had once known. She asked why he had abandoned his writing.

"Because I have written all there was to write," he responded. "I wrote when I did not know life, now that I know the meaning of life, I have no more to write."

Sites

Wilde's hotel

29, boulevard des Capucines (2nd arr.)
Métro: Opéra

In 1891, Wilde was again living in Paris, and this time it was his literary success—not his flamboyance and attention-getting antics—that made him the toast of the literary scene. It was at this address that Wilde began his play *Salomé*. One night, after relating the tale of Salomé to some other writers, he returned to his hotel and was suddenly inspired to write the story. But in the midst of writing he suddenly stopped and raced down to the Grand Café on the corner. He approached Rigo, the leader of the café's gypsy orchestra, and told him, "I am writing a play about a woman dancing with her bare feet in the blood of a man she has craved for and slain. I want you to play something in harmony with my thoughts."

Wilde later wrote, "And Rigo played such wild and terrible music that those who were there stopped talking and looked at each other with blanched faces. Then I went back and finished *Salomé*."

Hôtel d'Alsace (L'Hôtel)

13, rue des Beaux-Arts (6th arr.)
T: 01 44 41 99 00
www.l-hotel.com
Métro: St-Germain-des-Prés or Mabillon

In the summer of 1899, Wilde had wracked up so many debts that he was turned out of the Hôtel Marsollier (which still stands at 13, rue Marsollier, near the Louvre). Jean Duporier, the proprietor of the Hôtel d'Alsace, advanced the writer some money and took him in. Duporier treated Wilde just as well as—if not better than—his paying customers, each day bringing him a breakfast of coffee, bread, and butter at 11am, followed by a cutlet and two hardboiled eggs at 2pm. He also provided Wilde with a few bottles each week of Courvoisier, charging him less than thirty francs each.

Wilde died at the Hôtel d'Alsace on November 30, 1900. Guests at the four-star hotel may choose to sleep in Wilde's sumptuous quarters, which include emerald green walls, a swan masthead, and souvenirs of his stay there.

Père-Lachaise Cemetery

16 rue du Repos (20th arr.)
T: 01 55 25 82 10
Père-Lachaise is open daily 9am–5:30pm, with extended hours in the spring and summer. Entrance free.
www.pere-lachaise.com
Métro: Père-Lachaise, Gambetta, or Philippe-Auguste

> "He seems to have expressed a desire to be buried in Paris."
> "In Paris! I fear that hardly points to any very serious state of mind at the last."
> —*The Importance of Being Earnest*, 1895

The coffin was cheap, the horse worse for wear, and the gravestone a simple slab: the funeral of Oscar Wilde was third-rate by all accounts. The owner of Wilde's last residence, the Hôtel d'Alsace, provided a wreath *à mon locataire* (to my tenant), but otherwise there were as few flowers as there were mourners at Bagneux cemetery.

Less than a decade later, Wilde's body was removed from Bagneux and transported to Père-Lachaise, where the sculptor Jacob Epstein had been commissioned to create a memorial for him. The sculpture depicts a flying figure, half demon, half angel. Inscribed on the tomb is an excerpt from Wilde's last work, *The Ballad of Reading Gaol* (1898), written after his release from prison:

> And alien tears will fill for him
> Pity's long-broken urn,
> For his mourners will be outcast men,
> And outcasts always mourn.

A last-minute dispute between Epstein and Parisian officials resulted in a fig leaf bronze plaque being placed over the statue's genitalia. However, the problem was soon resolved by a group of well-meaning poets and students who, led by the occultist and poet Aleister Crowley, broke into the cemetery and stole the plaque.

Marcel Proust

(1871–1922)

I had always, within reach, a plan of Paris, which, because I could see drawn on it the street in which M. and Mme. Swann lived, seemed to me to contain a secret treasure.

—Marcel Proust
Swann's Way, 1913

On the snowy night of January 1, 1909, thirty-seven-year-old Marcel Proust returned to his home along 102, boulevard Haussmann to warm himself by the fire. His servant, Céleste, offered him a cup of tea. He dipped a madeleine into the cup and, upon tasting it, was flooded with memories of his uncle's garden in the western Parisian suburb of Auteuil, where Proust's grandfather had once fed him the little cakes soaked in tea.

Up until then, Proust had written only a few fanciful tales and a couple of unfinished novels and translations. But the sensation produced by the madeleine made him realize that the "materials of my literary work were my past life." It would become a key scene in the first volume of *In Search of Lost Time* (also translated as *Remembrance of Things Past*), in which the narrator, upon tasting one, is flooded with memories of Combray, the town of his youth.

Although *In Search of Lost Time* was not strictly autobiographical, it was based on the author's life, from his young days in the Auteuil garden and Paris's 17th arrondissement to his climb through Parisian society. It was also about the transformation of Paris's social landscape, in particular the decline of the aristocracy and rise of the middle class at the fin de siècle.

Born to a Jewish mother and Catholic father, Proust grew up in a comfortable, bourgeois environment near the parc Monceau. The family lived in a limestone building that still stands at 9, boulevard Malesherbes. What today is a chestnut-lined street with elegant homes was once, in Proust's eyes, "one of the ugliest districts in Paris."

Although Proust's father was an eminent doctor, the family lacked the prestige of Paris's oldest, noble families, many of whom lived in the 8th arrondissement and the section of the 7th arrondissement known as the Faubourg St.-Germain. Throughout his life—from his childhood on boulevard Malesherbes to his final home on the rue Hamelin—Proust cast a watchful eye toward that decadent, exclusive world, which would provide the setting for *In Search of Lost Time*:

> *The presence of the body of Jesus Christ in the sacrament seemed to me no more obscure a mystery than this leading house in the Faubourg being situated on the right bank of the river and so near that from my bedroom in*

the morning I could hear its carpets being beaten. But the line of demarcation that separated me from the Faubourg Saint-Germain seemed to me all the more real because it was purely ideal.

At that time, a half-Jewish homosexual such as Proust would not have had easy access to that world. But Proust found a way in, with the help of a few wealthy school friends and the well-connected Symbolist poet Robert de Montesquiou, who repaid Proust's sycophantic devotion with introductions to society's most sought-after women.

Proust's visits to them provided many of the personalities that would fill the pages of *In Search of Lost Time*. At 12, avenue Hoche stood the home of Madame Arman, whose salon was dominated by her lover, the writer Anatole France—who would later be the inspiration for Proust's character Bergotte. A character based on Princess Mathilde Bonaparte would appear in Proust's novel, thanks to their lively conversations at her salon at 20, rue de Berry. Madame Lemaire's salons were nearby at 3, rue de Monceau, while on the rue Dumont-d'Urville, Proust met Laure

Hayman, the inspiration for one of his most famous characters—the beautiful but dim-witted Odette de Crécy. Central, too, was the rue d'Astorg, where Madame Aubernon's salon provided Proust with a model for his fictional Madame Verdurin, a "thoroughly virtuous woman who came of a respectable middle-class family excessively rich and wholly undistinguished," and her salon, where "every Wednesday, and indeed every day, the most various and interesting people and the smartest women in Paris stood out."

Proust's characters frequented the finest of Parisian establishments, many of which are still around today: the Café de la Paix (12, boulevard des Capucines), where high society headed after the masked balls; the coffee and pastry shop Ladurée at 16, rue Royale, which was one of Odette de Crécy's "smart places;" and the jeweler Boucheron (26, place Vendôme), where Robert de St.-Loup agonized over the purchase of a necklace for his lover.

Proust eventually found a publisher for his work, the first volume of which was greeted with great critical

enthusiasm in 1913. The writer now found himself the subject of new attention from Parisian society, but he had become increasingly reclusive, and preferred to stay in his room at 102, boulevard Haussmann. He requested that his friends visit him only at night, in part because he had acquired a phobia of sunlight.

Proust had moved to the second-floor apartment in 1906, following the death of his mother. The apartment, which was previously occupied by his uncle, was the "triumph of bad bourgeois taste," and "the ugliest thing I ever saw. . . . Frightful dust, trees under and against my window, the noise of the boulevard between the Printemps and Saint-Augustin." He lined his room with cork to block out noise and kept his windows shut. The air was often thick with inhalants, which he took to treat his asthma.

Despite his reclusion, Proust could still be spotted on the town—and often from a distance, as his fur coat, white face, and black-rimmed eyes produced an effect hard to miss. He began dining at the Ritz several times a week, eventually acquiring the nickname "Proust of the Ritz." In *In Search of Lost Time*, Proust would later recall American women during World War I "hugging to their bursting breasts pearl necklaces which would buy them a 'busted' duke. On such nights, the Hotel Ritz must resemble an exchange and mart emporium."

Proust also became a frequent visitor at the Hôtel Marigny, then at 11, rue de l'Arcade. The Hôtel Marigny was, in fact, a male brothel, and Proust had helped its owner, a former royal footman, purchase the hotel in 1917. From the Malesherbes apartment he had shared with his parents for thirty years, he furnished the Hôtel Marigny with chairs, sofas, and carpets that were, as he described in *In Search of Lost Time*, "tortured by the cruel contact to which I had delivered them without defense!"

In 1919, Proust's boulevard Haussmann building was sold to the bank Varin-Bernier (today it is marked by a plaque). Forced to leave, Proust sold his cork walls to a manufacturer of bottle corks and moved first to a thin-walled "house made of paper" at 8, *bis* rue Laurent-Pichat, then to 44, rue Hamelin, a narrow, shadowy street between the Arc de Triomphe and the Trocadéro. Despite the prestigious location, Proust's fifth-floor apartment

was little more than "a vile hovel just large enough for my bedstead." He gave the children on the floor above him felt slippers so that they would not make too much noise and began working on the proofs of his next volume, *The Guermantes Way*.

The Guermantes Way, published in May 1921, would be Proust's final work. The author had been announcing his imminent death since 1905 and his asthma, combined with years of narcotic and stimulant abuse, finally caught up with him. He died on November 18, 1922.

Sites

The Cave of Ali Baba
41, quai d'Orsay (7th arr.)
Métro: Invalides

Count Montesquiou lived in the attic, in his "Cave of Ali Baba," in a sprawling building emblazoned with his family's coat of arms and a large "M" above the entrance. The Montesquiou-Fézensac family was descended from the first dynasty of French kings and had the building constructed in 1863 in their honor.

Although some found him a bore, Montesquiou represented for Proust a path to the loftiest circles of the Faubourg St.-Germain. Proust pumped the count for gossip and introductions, and later made him into the evil Baron Chalrus in *In Search of Lost Time*. Montesquoiu mocked Proust's work when its first volume was published, calling *Swann's Way* a "hodgepodge of litanies and lechery."

The Bois de Boulogne

Pavillon d'Armenonville
Allée de Longchamp (16th arr.)
T: 01 40 67 93 00
Métro: Porte Maillot

Proust—like his characters—was a frequent visitor to the Bois de Boulogne. The Bois was a frequent Sunday destination for society women: the real-life Madeleine Lemaire held teas at the Chalet des Îles; Proust's fictional Madame Verdurin set her summer dinner parties there; and Odette took daily walks there, strolling past admiring men in her plumed hats and lilac skirts, "dressed as the populace imagined queens to be dressed."

At the Armenonville restaurant, Swann and Odette listened to the "little phrase" of music that would become a recurring motif in *In Search of Lost Time*. Each time Swann heard the sonata he thought of the Bois, with its "moonlight preventing the leaves from moving."

Today the Bois remains true to the forest-like park that Proust described as having the

> . . . temporary, unfinished, artificial look of a nursery garden or a park in which, either for some botanic purpose or in preparation for a festival, there have been embedded among the trees . . . a few rare specimens . . . which seem to be clearing all around themselves an empty space.

Located at Paris's western edge, the Bois is a popular weekend destination for Parisians. The Pavillon has recently been restored.

Bibliothèque Mazarine

23, quai de Conti (6th arr.)
T: 01 44 41 44 06
Open Monday to Friday 10am–6pm
www.bibliotheque-mazarine.fr
Métro: Pont-Neuf, Louvre-Rivoli, or Odéon

Proust's parents, hoping their twenty-four-year old son would pursue a respectable job, helped him acquire a job as an honorary assistant at the Bibliothèque Mazarine.

Although unpaid, the position was prestigious: the library, opened in 1643, is the oldest public library in France. The workload was minimal; Proust was only required to work five hours per day, for at least two days per week. Yet he was rarely seen between his hiring in July 1895 and that fall. Nevertheless, in December he applied for a year's leave.

The Mazarine remains one of France's prized literary and scientific research libraries, boasting an impressive collection of illuminated manuscripts and bookbindings.

Jardin des Plantes

57, rue Cuvier (5th arr.)
T: 01 40 79 30 00
Open daily
Métro: Austerlitz-Jussieu

In 1913, Proust was considering *Colombes Poignardées* (*Bleeding-Heart Pigeons*) as the title for the second volume of *In Search of Lost Time*.

The idea had been inspired by a walk taken nearly two decades earlier in the Jardin des Plantes, Paris's botanical garden created in 1577 and developed by Louis XIII in the seventeenth century. Proust and his friends were taken by the *colombes poignardées*, a species of pigeon with a red spot on its chest. "They look like nymphs who have stabbed themselves for love, and some god has changed them into birds," said Proust's companion.

Proust later abandoned the title for two new ones, *In the Shadow of Young Girls in Flower* and *The Guermantes Way*.

Giovanni Boldini: *Count Robert de Montesquiou*, 1897.
Musee d'Orsay, Paris/Lauros/Giraudon/Bridgeman Art Library.

Colette

(1873–1954)

Of course I can't conceive that people live in Paris for pleasure, of their own free will, but I do begin to understand that one can get interested in what goes on in these huge six-storied boxes.

—Colette
Claudine in Paris, 1901

Reutlinger Studio: Colette acting in *Rêve d'Égypt*, 1907.

Private Collection. Archives Charmet/Bridgeman Art Library.

In the fall of 1906, Paris was abuzz with the latest production at L'Olympia, the famed theater still standing near the Opéra on the boulevard des Capucines. All about town, posters were advertising *The Gypsy*, an upcoming production starring a blonde *provocatrice* named Colette. As the premiere approached, rumors flew that Colette had fled Paris and was now living *la vie bohème* with a group of gypsies in the country.

But when the curtain rose on October 1, Colette was on stage, "a capricious and wild bohemian," recalled one critic, "scantily dressed in rags that barely hide her white nudity."

That Colette would take to the stage nearly nude came as little surprise to those who knew her well. Most everything about Gabrielle Gauthier-Villars—who called herself Colette—exuded a liberated air. She dressed in multicolored scarves and felt hats, and rolled her "r's" in an exotic manner. She filled her luxurious home at 177, rue de Courcelles with paintings, photographs, and sculptures of herself, and held regular gatherings at which members of high society found themselves alongside poets and transvestites.

To regular Parisians, she was best known simply as Colette Willy, the wife of the journalist Henry "Willy" Gauthier-Villars, and author of the *Claudine* novels. The series of novels, which Colette had ghostwritten under her husband's name, were about the new life that a young woman from the provinces makes for herself in Paris. Colette filled the books with typical Parisian characters and sites, such as "that little pub in the Avenue Trudaine—the one with the shady but extremely affable proprietor."

The *Claudine* books also included several homosexual scenes, which scandalized Parisians and had many rushing to buy the line of Claudine-brand products that Colette had created, from cosmetics and perfume to ice cream and chocolates.

As their fame grew, Henry and Colette mingled with both bohemians and the wealthy in the finest salons and gambling houses, and each took several lovers. Although Colette and Henry's various affairs were closely followed by the press, few were prepared for the news that appeared in the papers shortly after Colette's appearance in *The Gypsy* in 1906: the actress and writer of "wild manners and gests" had moved out of the home she shared with Henry on the rue de Courcelles and taken an apartment at 44, rue de Villejust, near the apartment of her latest lover, Mathilde, the daughter of the Duke of Morny, Napoleon III's half-brother. Mathilde de Morny, or "Missy," as Colette called her, was dubbed "Uncle Max" by her friends for her preference for masculine dress.

While her personal life made waves in the Parisian papers, Colette took to the stage once again, and she and Mathilde began going to the music halls and shadier bars along the rue de la Gaîté, which attracted people from the margins of Parisian society: *cocottes*, gigolos, bisexuals, and music hall dancers who were "never averse to a skimpy costume or a kitschy production." Colette's novel *The Vagabond* (1910) revealed the goings-on in this bohemian world, where actresses at fine theaters such as the Comédie-Française became the whores at the Jockey Club after hours.

Colette's relationship with Mathilde ended in 1911 and the following year she married Henry de Jouvenal, the editor-in-chief of the newspaper *Le Matin*. Colette filled Henry's Swiss-style chalet on the rue Cortambert with cats, dogs, snakes, lizards, and a Brazilian squirrel named Ricotte. But as her husband ascended the political ladder, he found that his infamous wife was a liability, and the marriage did not last.

Colette found Paris to be a banal, "filthy place," yet she always returned to the city after a tour in the provinces, and lived in fourteen homes in the city during her lifetime. Her descriptions of Paris were always precise and evocative. The rue du Mont Thabor, with its ancient houses, was the "sad verso of the sunny Rue de Rivoli." The rue Royale was a stretch of "newsvendors and shopgirls, flanked by jade necklaces and silver-fox furs." Auteuil, on the edges of western Paris, was for "those in flight from the crowds and the noise of the city." Behind the walls in Montmartre, "gardens were dozing, each dotted with saucers of food for the cats, tumble-down summer-houses, and little, starved-looking currant bushes."

When World War I swept Paris, Colette refused to hide in the cellar with her neighbors—a sex-crazed concierge, a newspaper editor, and a deaf countess. Instead, when the sirens began to roar, she opened the windows of her Palais-Royal apartment and gazed down onto the square below. That same window would provide the inspiration for *Paris from My Window* (1942), Colette's account of the city during the Occupation and of her world in the "the deep and fragile buildings of the Palais-Royal."

Crippled by arthritis, Colette spent her last years surrounded by her cats in the Palais-Royal, transported from one place to another atop a divan from which she greeted those who came to pay their respects. Among them was Simone de Beauvoir, who wrote:

Arthritic, wild-haired, violently made-up, age gave [Colette's] sharp face and her blue eyes an electric brilliance: between her collection of paperweights and the gardens framed by her windows, she appeared, paralyzed and sovereign, like a formidable Mother-Goddess.

Sites

Palais-Royal

9, rue de Beaujolais (1st arr.)
Today the Palais-Royal is home to the
State Council, the Constitutional
Council, and the Ministry of Culture.
Métro: Palais-Royal

It was 6:30am on December 12, 1941,
when the German police knocked at
the second-floor apartment of 9, rue
de Beaujolais. Brandishing guns, they
seized Colette's Jewish third husband,
Maurice Goudeket. Maurice was taken
to a camp near Compiègne, and it was
not until next February that Colette's
powerful connections secured his
release. When Maurice returned, he
refused to sleep in the apartment and
would instead spend the night in a
maid's room two floors up.

In the nineteenth century, the
Palais-Royal was home to the gambling
houses and brothels made famous in
the works of Balzac. But in the twentieth century it became a refuge for
artists, and its licentious dives gave
way to gardens, shops, and old men
feeding birds. Colette wrote lovingly
of the area, its "Louvre and its flower
beds, Rivoli and its arcades." Colette's
main windows looked onto the Palais-

Royal, and from her perch she could
communicate with her neighbors and
friends, the poet Jean Cocteau, the
painter Christian Bérard, and the composer Mireille Hartuch.

Colette lived at the Palais-Royal
until her death in 1954.

The Salon of Nathalie Barney

20, rue Jacob (6th arr.)
Métro: St.-Germain-des-Prés

Colette had long expressed an interest
in acting, and finally, in 1905, her
friend, and former lover, Nathalie
Clifford Barney, provided her the opportunity. Nathalie, said Colette, was a
beautiful, wealthy American with "sea-
blue eyes" who seduced many Parisian
society women and recorded her con-
quests in a little book.

Nathalie kept a property in Neuilly,
near the Bois de Boulogne, which she
often lent to her love interests. In June
she held a garden party there and
allowed Colette to perform a pan-
tomime with Nathalie's current lover.
Although the act was well received, the
real showstopper came when a nearly
nude woman rode into the garden upon
a white, bejeweled horse. The woman
was Mata Hari, the Dutch exotic dancer
turned spy who would later be shot by
the French.

For nearly sixty years, Nathalie held
her garden parties in a home along the
rue Jacob, the same street where in
past centuries Cardinal Richelieu, Jean
Racine, and Honoré de Balzac had
met their mistresses. Guests passed
through a Greek temple at the bottom
of her garden, on whose Doric columns
she had engraved "A l'amitié." She
sometimes had the path strewn with
rose petals.

Among her guests were Ezra
Pound, T.S. Eliot, Sherwood Anderson,
Marcel Proust, James Joyce, and
Guillaume Apollinaire. She wrote sev-
eral works, including *Thoughts of an
Amazon*, and outlived most everyone,
dying in 1972, a few years shy of one
hundred.

La Gaîté Montparnasse

26, rue de la Gaîté (14th arr.)
T: 01 43 22 16 18
www.gaite.com
Métro: Gaîté or Edgar Quinet

In 1913, while Colette was touring
France as a music-hall performer, she
stopped in Paris to perform *The Flesh*,
one of her most famous roles.

Colette and Missy.
Collection Jouvenel / Centre d'études Colette.

On the rue de la Gaîté, the smell of crêpes, *gauffres*, and oysters wafted down the street, past the Théâtre de la Gaîté Montparnasse, whose rococo façade was adorned with grimacing masks. Theatergoers waited with anticipation for the doors to open.

"There are few popular establishments so frequented by the milk maids bored of selling their cheeses, the clueless grocer boys . . . the gentlemen in their caps," wrote the journalist Henry de Forge upon seeing Colette's performance. The mixed clientele was unique for a Parisian theater, and in return for a handful of *sous* one received an "ineffable chicken coop armchair, cramped and poorly stuffed, in the midst of an atmosphere in which the odor of tobacco, oranges, and more subtle smells mixed agreeably."

The theater is still open today.

Moulin-Rouge

82, boulevard de Clichy (18th arr.)
T: 01 53 09 82 82
www.moulinrouge.fr
Métro: Blanche

During the final weeks of 1906, the de Morny family crest appeared on a Moulin-Rouge publicity poster for *Rêve d'Égypte*. The director's provocative act did not go unnoticed. Everyone knew that the piece, about an Egyptologist who falls in love with a mummy, would star Colette. But no member of the nobility wanted to believe that Mathilde "Missy" de Morny —related to Napoleon III—would appear on stage with Colette, who had been her lover since the previous year.

On January 3, 1907, as the curtain fell on the opening night, Colette's husband, Henry, readied himself for the worst. Missy had just played the Egyptologist to Colette's mummy, and the outrage was unanimous.

"*Cocu! Cocu!*" yelled some. Others came at Henry and his mistress with their canes and fists. The two narrowly escaped thanks to some effective elbowing and the quick appearance of security gaurds.

These were not any ordinary theater ruffians but rather the nobility, which had turned out in force to see one of their own—Mathilde, the Marquise de Morny—act alongside her lover.

The scandal surrounding *Rêve d'Égypte* was so great that the production soon came to an end.

Colette at the window of her apartment at the Palais-Royal, date unknown.

Gertrude Stein

(1874–1946)

All roads lead to Paris.

—Gertrude Stein, 1933

Leo Stein was already living near the Luxembourg Gardens when his sister Gertrude arrived in Paris in 1903. Within a short time, the Steins were collecting art by the likes of Cézanne and Picasso, and enchanting many of Paris's young artists and writers at their Montparnasse apartment at 27, rue de Fleurus. Their Saturday night salon, Gertrude later recalled, drew "geniuses, near geniuses, and might be geniuses," including the writers Guillaume Apollinaire and Mina Loy and the artists Pablo Picasso, Henri Matisse, Georges Braque, and Juan Gris, who came for the good food and conversation—and of course, to see their works hanging on the Stein wall. Gertrude knew how to play to their vanity:

> You know how painters are, I wanted to make them happy so I placed each one opposite his own picture, and they were so happy that we had to send out twice for more bread, when you know France you will know that means they were happy, because they cannot eat and drink without bread and we had to send out twice for more bread so they were happy.

Although firmly ensconced in Parisian life, Stein, who had quit her medical studies in favor of a literary career, looked primarily to America for her subject matter. One of her more ambitious projects was *The Making of Americans* (1925), a fictionalized, 1,000-page history of her family and, she declared, "the whole world." She became so immersed in her project, and in the connections between people, that, "when I used to go down the streets of Paris I wondered whether they were people I knew or ones I didn't."

In 1913, Leo moved out, leaving Gertrude with the Picasso paintings and her lover, Alice B. Toklas. Stein—"Pussy"—was short and round, Toklas—"Lovey"—was wiry and stylish (Ernest Hemingway's wife Hadley called her "an amiable gargoyle"). Their relationship spanned nearly four decades. When Picasso and Matisse (and later Hemingway and Ford Madox Ford) came to visit, they were directed to Stein, their wives to Toklas.

When the war came, Stein and Toklas fled the Zeppelin raids on Paris and headed to Spain. "She thought neither of manuscripts nor of pictures, she thought only of Paris and she was desolate," Stein later wrote of the period. In 1917, Stein acquired a Ford van so that she and Toklas could help supply hospitals in Perpignan and Nîmes. Their support earned them the French government's *Médaille de la Reconnaissance Française.*

It was a changed Paris that they returned to in May 1919. The streets were suddenly filled again with young men—new men, said Gertrude, not the ones she knew. Her friend Guillaume Apollinaire had died following an injury in the war, and Stein and Toklas suspended their salon to save money.

But a fresh batch of Americans had arrived in Paris and new faces soon filled the ground-floor apartment, including those of Sherwood Anderson, Ernest Hemingway, F. Scott Fitzgerald, Robert McAlmon, and Ford Madox Ford. The tradition of Stein's old salon would be replaced in the 1920s by this "lost generation" (a term later attributed to Gertrude but that she claimed was told to her by a French hotel keeper).

Stein, now approaching fifty, was known to some of these young writers as the "mother of us all," in part for her role as a mentor. She helped reshape Hemingway's early stories, advising him to forget weighty meditations on Paris or art. "Hemingway," she said, "remarks are not literature."

Yet while disciples like Hemingway flourished, Stein struggled for recognition of her own. In addition to poetry and stories, she tried her hand at libretti and a film script in French. But outside her Montparnasse circle, Stein was considered a cryptic writer—as is suggested by her most famous statement, "A rose is a rose is a rose."

In 1933, at age fifty-nine, Stein finally had her first commercial success with *The Autobiography of Alice B. Toklas,* a gossipy book relating Stein's life through the voice of her lover. Americans loved it, Parisian intellectuals laughed at it, and some of her friends broke with her because of it. The book was full of half-truths and apocryphal tales about Stein and her Parisian circle, some of whom felt slighted by her anecdotes. Following the book's publication, the magazine *Transition* even published a booklet, *Testimony Against Gertrude Stein* in which the artists Braque, Matisse, and Tristan Tzara listed Stein's alleged untruths. "Miss Stein understood nothing of what went on around her.

But no superegoist does. . . . She never went beyond the state of tourists," wrote Braque.

In 1938, Stein and Toklas left their Montparnasse apartment to move to St.-Germain, settling in a seventeenth-century building that still stands at 5, rue Christine. Their apartment was just around the corner from Picasso's studio, at 7, rue des Grands-Augustins. St.-Germain, now a fashionable, upscale neighborhood, was a contrast to the Montmartre studios and ateliers Picasso and Stein had frequented in earlier years:

> Now we all live in the ancient quarter near the river, now that the twentieth century is decided and has its characters we all tend to want to live in seventeenth century houses, not barracks of ateliers as we did then . . . we need the picturesque the splendid we need the air and space you only get in old quarters.

But their stay here was brief. As Stein's latest work, *Paris France,* hit bookstands, the Germans occupied

Gertrude Stein and Alice B. Toklas with their godson John "Bumby" Hemingway in Paris. Photo EH 6886P. The John F. Kennedy Library.

Paris. Stein and Toklas, both Jewish, left the city, and while the Gestapo raided their Paris apartment, the two survived in the countryside with the help of a vegetable garden. They did not consider fleeing to the US. A few years before, in *An American and France*, Stein had written,

> America is my country and Paris is my home town and it is as it has come to be. After all anybody is as their land and air is. Anybody is as the sky is low or high, the air heavy or clean and anybody is as there is wind or no wind there. It is that which makes them and the arts they make and the work they do and the way they eat and the way they drink and the way they learn and everything.

Stein died in July 1946 at the age of seventy-two and was buried at Père-Lachaise. Her tombstone misspells her birthplace and misstates the date of her death.

Sites

Stein's former residence

27, rue de Fleurus (6th arr.)
Métro: St.-Placide or Rennes

First-time visitors to Stein's Montparnasse home were not often impressed as they approached the building at 27, rue de Fleurus. Although there were certainly wealthy homes to be found in the quarter, this one seemed neither chic nor charming. A shabby courtyard was followed by an equally shabby concierge's loge. To the right was Stein's garden-floor apartment.

It was only after Stein or Toklas opened their door that the visitor's impression changed. The apartment was luxurious, filled with Italian Renaissance–style furniture. Paintings were hung as high as the ceiling, while uncomfortable but stately looking chairs awaited. Toklas had tea and pastries ready for the guest. And then there was Stein, seated in her high-backed chair:

> She peacefully let her legs hang . . . and when any one of the many visitors came to ask her a question she lifted herself up out of this chair and usually replied in French, not just now.

Stein and Toklas preferred hosting at their home to meeting with friends at the cafés of Montparnasse or St.-Germain. "It wasn't café conversation at the rue de Fleurus so there was no need to continue it at cafés," Toklas remarked.

It was at this same home that the Stein siblings held their salons after Getrude's arrival in 1903 and that Picasso and Matisse first became acquainted. It was also here that, Stein, seated across from Cézanne's *Portrait of Madame Cézanne*, began one of her most famous works, a collection of stories based not in France but in America: *Three Lives* (1906).

In 1937, the 27, rue de Fleurus landlord refused to renew Stein's lease, and Stein and Toklas were forced to move. "I guess 27 got so historical, it just could not hold us any longer," Stein wrote. Stein's home still stands, and today a plaque commemorates the more than thirty years she spent here. She is one of the few Americans to ever receive such an honor from the French.

Picasso's studio

7, rue des Grands-Augustins (6th arr.)
Metro: St.-Michel

The first Pablo Picasso painting acquired by the Stein siblings was *Girl with a Basket of Flowers*, which they purchased in 1905. Leo immediately liked the painting, but Gertrude did not take to Picasso's rendition of the girl's feet and legs. The dealer, an ex-clown named Clovis Sagot, was quick to accommodate, saying "If you do not like the legs and feet it is very easy to guillotine her and only take the head." The Steins turned his proposition down and finally agreed to purchase the painting for 150 francs (about $30).

Picasso and Stein got along wonderfully. She was enthusiastic about his increasingly abstract approach to painting (which would soon lead him to Cubism). Inspired by his work, Stein later attempted to adapt Cubist concepts to writing.

Although Picasso's fame had eclipsed Stein's by the 1930s, the two remained good friends. In 1937, Picasso moved his studio (and eventually his home) to 7, rue des Grands-Augustins, just a few streets away from Stein's home on 5, rue de Christine. The following year, Stein published *Picasso*, a book about the painter.

The seventeenth-century *hôtel particulier* was a step up from Picasso's old Montmartre studio, in the Bâteau-Lavoir where he had painted Stein's portrait years before. The house, which had been the setting of Balzac's *The Unknown Masterpiece*, was a maze of rooms and passageways cluttered with books, bird cages, and artwork. It was here that he painted *Guernica*.

Guillaume Apollinaire

(1880–1918)

Ah! What a charming thing

To leave a dreary place

For Paris

Lovely Paris

Which once Love must have created.

—Guillame Apollinaire,
date unknown

On April 25, 1903, at a small café on the place St.-Michel, twenty-two-year-old Guillaume Apollinaire (Guglielmo de Kostrowitzky) made his literary debut. The poet André Salmon accompanied him that night:

> *Apollinaire stood up, heavily. . . . From his mouth he removed a little white clay pipe decorated in black, green, and red. . . . Looking somber, almost angry, a bit of reddish moustache half-hiding an almost feminine pout, he walked straight to the piano, leaned firmly against it, and began to declaim vehemently, in an intense, low-pitched voice, the poem "Schinderhannes."*

Apollinaire's audience was a hodgepodge of bohemians, students, and young writers. Upon hearing his poem, some turned up their noses, but others were immediately impressed. The influence of the rich imagery of Verlaine, Rimbaud, and Mallarmé was evident, and yet there was clearly something very new in the verse Apollinaire recited that night at the café and published in his poetry review, *Le Festin d'Ésope*:

> *On Paris balconies the flowers*
> *Lean like so many Pisan towers,*
> *A barrel-organ sobs below.*
> *Eternity, instead of hours,*
> *Is Sundays like this in a row.*
> *The nights in Paris all drink gin*
> *And fall asleep with their streetlights*
> *   on.*
> *Trolley cars are mad machines*
> *To make green sparks and scream*
> *   like queens.*

Apollinaire was the bridge between traditional poetry and modernity. His Paris was a collage of quotidian scenes, glimpses of the city's changing look and pace, and the setting for the poet's own defeats and victories: "Anywhere but in Paris I / Would have the heart this month to die," he once wrote.

Born in Rome and raised in Monaco, Apollinaire had moved to Paris in 1889, living with his mother and working as a bank clerk. He did not know his father—he variously claimed to be the son of a prince, a pope, and a heretic. Friends knew not to take him too seriously. He was known to walk through Paris and announce with an expert air the value of a Parisian monument or a shabby building, and for a year before World

War I, he pretended to be a woman, Louise Lalanne, and reviewed the work of other female poets under her name. He also composed a list of all nine hundred works in the collection of erotica and sexology in the Bibliothèque Nationale, bribing an employee to bring him and his friends three illicit works at a time.

Most were charmed by the poet. Pablo Picasso met him in Fox's Bar (then at 26, rue d'Amsterdam), and was so impressed that a few days later he brought along his good friend the poet Max Jacob, who later recalled the encounter:

Apollinaire was smoking a short-stemmed pipe and expatiating on Petronius and Nero to some rather vulgar-looking people whom I took to be jobbers of some kind or traveling salesmen. He was wearing a stained light-colored suit, and a tiny straw hat was perched atop his famous pear-shaped head. He had hazel eyes, terrible and gleaming, a bit of curly blond hair fell over his forehead, his mouth looked like a little pimento, he had strong limbs, a broad chest looped across by a platinum watch-chain, and a ruby on his finger.

The three became inseparable, and Apollinaire's circle soon included not just poets and writers but also several painters—in particular, the Cubists. Apollinaire became their greatest promoter, writing several enthusiastic pieces about Cubism, inspired by his discussions with Picasso, Braque, Gris, Léger, and Picabia, among others. Although many of the Cubists would later attack Apollinaire's lack of artistic understanding, few denied his passion for their work.

Apollinaire brought Cubism to the written page. In poems such as "Lundi Rue Christine," a collection of conversations overheard in a Left Bank bar, he imbued poetry with the Cubist perspective of simultaneity and multiplicity. He also created *calligrammes*— poems in the shape of everyday objects, such as guitars or other forms used by the Cubists in their paintings.

The years before World War I were the height of Apollinaire's friendship with Picasso and Jacob, filled with poetry readings at the Closerie des Lilas, opium smoking in a Montmartre or Left Bank apartment, and long nights at the Lapin Agile, the Lipp, and the Rotonde.

But in 1911 Apollinaire was arrested in connection with the disap-

pearance of the *Mona Lisa*. Although his name was eventually cleared, he was humiliated. Soon after his trial, his girlfriend, the painter Marie Laurencin, ended their relationship.

Not used to seeing him so glum, Apollinaire's friends dreamed up a new literary magazine, *Les Soirées de Paris*, which for a time was one of the premier avant-garde literary reviews in France. During this same period, he published his poetry collection *Alcools, Poèmes 1898–1913*, which many today consider to be his finest work. Haunted by memories of Laurencin, he left Auteuil—"charming quarter of my great sorrows"—for the lively clubs and cafés of St.-Germain, settling just steps away from the Café Flore, which he frequented and which still stands.

As a foreigner, Apollinaire was under no obligation to join the French forces fighting in World War I, but his desire to be recognized as a Frenchman and to redeem his name after the *Mona Lisa* scandal led him to enlist. He took a liking to his new profession, declaring to his friends that it was all "smoking parties, cocaine . . . an artificial paradise." But in March 1916, just a few days after he was awarded French nationality, he was wounded in the head by shell splinters.

The trepanation performed on the poet left him violent and prone to sudden outbursts of anger, but he continued to write. He subtitled his play *The Breasts of Tirésias* "*drame surréaliste*," a mysterious new term that soon reappeared in a program he wrote for Jean Cocteau's ballet *Parade*. With music composed by Eric Satie, and costumes by Picasso, the event typified this new term, which described something dreamlike and not entirely real. It was a concept that was soon embraced by a young generation of artists such as André Breton and Louis Aragon, who became known as the Surrealists.

Although he was approaching forty, Apollinaire had become the embodiment of all that was new and fresh in art—not just for the future school of Surrealists but also for the Dadaists, who published a poem by Apollinaire in their *Cabaret Voltaire* review in 1916. But just two years later Apollinaire was dead. His war wound had left him vulnerable, and his body could not combat what should have been a mild ailment.

Anonymous: Portrait of Marie Laurencin, 1908.

Private Collection, Paris, France. © Snark/Art Resource, NY.

His good friend Picasso was shaving before his hotel mirror when word reached him of Apollinaire's death. Struck by the news, he stopped shaving and looked into the mirror. He was so taken by the extraordinary sadness of his expression that he picked up a pencil and sketched what is said to be the last self-portrait he ever made.

Sites

Café du Départ

1, place St.-Michel (6th arr.)
T: 01 43 54 24 55
Métro: St.-Michel

Saturday nights at 9pm, the cellar of the Café du Départ began to fill with smoke and the loud voices of students and poets representing all of Paris's artistic schools—from Parnassians, Symbolists, and Decadists to Brutalists, Magi, Kabbalists, and Instrumentalists. Above, the main café was nearly empty, but below one hundred to one hundred fifty young men were packed into the long, narrow cellar, at the end of which was a makeshift stage.

The Saturday night gatherings, hosted by *La Plume* literary review, had begun in 1889, and were for a time frequented by Paul Verlaine—whose recitations were often the highlight of the event despite his drunkenness and increasingly weakened state.

The gatherings ended after six years, but were resurrected in 1902. *La Plume* announced that only those bearing invitations would be admitted. Instead, said Apollinaire's friend André Salmon, "Not only did nobody ask to

see your card, but if you had the naiveté to show it to the café proprietor or one of his waiters it was looked at with curiosity and suspicion."

Apollinaire was in attendance from nearly the beginning, and made his poetry debut alongside the ramshackle piano on April 25, 1903. Although not all audience members were enthusiastic, his recitation caught the attention of *La Plume*, which soon published the young poet's verses.

But Apollinaire and Salmon tired of the bohemian crowd at the Saturday soirées. In what Salmon later called his "torn-trousers snobbery," Apollinaire began to wear his most raggedy clothes to the events, slighting his peers and their Bohemian outfits.

When the soirées finally came to an end, Apollinaire blamed their demise on the Café du Départ: "This melancholy name probably hastened the end of the soirées, and probably the end of *La Plume* itself: the name was an invitation to travel, and it made us all take our leave quite quickly."

In the days prior to the reconstruction of the quai St.-Michel, the café's

Guillaume Apollinaire: *"L'Horloge de Demain,"* calligram published in Issue #4 of *391* (color litho).
Bibliothèque Litteraire Jacques Doucet, Paris, France. Archives Charmet/Bridgeman Art Library.

L'HORLOGE DE DEMAIN

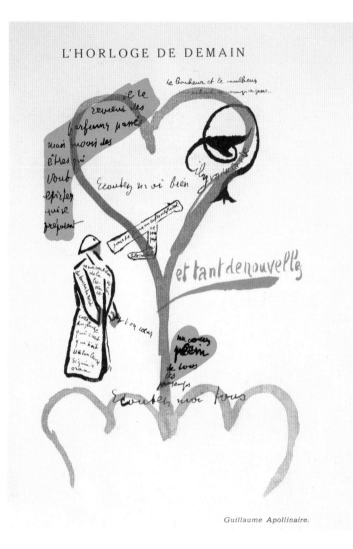

Guillaume Apollinaire.

cellar looked out onto the river. Today only the main floor of the café is open for business.

Le Bâteau-Lavoir
13, place Emile-Goudeau (18th arr.)
Métro: Abbesses

At about the same time there was living in Montmartre a youth with searching eyes whose face was reminiscent at once of Raphael and Forain. Pablo Picasso. . . . He was living in that strange wooden house in the Rue Ravignan [today the place Emile-Goudeau] which was inhabited by so many artists famous today or in the way of becoming so. I met him there in 1905. His reputation had not yet spread beyond the boundaries of the Butte. His blue workman's blouse, his occasionally cruel quips, the strangeness of his art, were the talk of Montmartre. His studio, cluttered with canvases representing mystical harlequins and drawings on which people walked and which everyone was allowed to carry off with him, was the meeting place of all the young artists, all the young poets.

When Apollinaire first met Picasso, the painter was living with his mistress, Fernande Olivier, in a lopsided, dilapi-dated building. The building was known as the Bâteau-Lavoir ("the laundry barge"), named for its resemblance to the floating wash sheds in the Seine used by French laundresses.

Apollinaire spent several evenings at the Bâteau-Lavoir, often arriving with books and engravings he had purchased during his walks in Paris. Sometimes he recited his poems ("He was very bad at it," said Olivier); other times he was content to calmly smoke his pipe alongside Picasso.

Down the street was Picasso's devoted poet friend Max Jacob, whom Picasso soon introduced to Apollinaire. According to Olivier, it was at the Bâteau-Lavoir that the three men did "nothing but quarrel . . . and exchange curses." Jacob had a different memory: he later called the period of his friendship with Picasso and Apollinaire "the best days of my life."

Picasso lived at this apartment from 1904 to 1909. Although the building burned down in 1970, it was replaced with a concrete replica.

Musée du Louvre
36, quai du Louvre (1st arr.)
T: 1 40 20 53 17
The Louvre is open daily, except Tuesdays and certain public holidays, 9am–6pm. Open until 9:45pm on Wednesdays and Fridays.
www.louvre.fr
Métro: Palais-Royal / Musée du Louvre

Most Parisian newspapers ran a similar headline on August 23, 1911:
MONA LISA GONE FROM THE LOUVRE

Rumors flew about the city as to the painting's whereabouts. Apollinaire and Picasso took the disappearance seriously. A few years before, Apollinaire's secretary, Géry Pieret, had stolen two statues from the Louvre:

"I'm going to the Louvre," he had announced to Marie Laurencin. "Can I bring you anything?"

That evening Pieret returned home carrying two Iberian stone sculptures he had stolen from the museum. In need of money, he sold them to Picasso, who found inspiration in them for his latest painting, *Les Demoiselles*

The original Bâteau-Lavoir in Montmartre.
© Roger-Viollet.

d'Avignon. In 1911, no longer employed by Apollinaire, he turned up again in Paris and stole yet another statue. A few days later, the disappearance of the *Mona Lisa* was announced.

Apollinaire and Picasso worried that Pieret was behind the *Mona Lisa* theft and decided they should dump the statues in the Seine after midnight to rid themselves of any incriminating evidence.

"I must say that although I shared their fears I had been watching them rather carefully that night," wrote Picasso's mistress, Fernande Olivier. "I am sure that perhaps involuntarily they had been play-acting a little—to such a point that although neither of them knew anything about cards, while they had sat waiting for the fatal moment when they would set out for the Seine—'the moment of the crime' —they had pretended to play cards all evening, doubtless in imitation of certain bandits they had read about."

Instead, the men spent the night wandering the Paris streets, so paranoid that they were unable to find a good moment to dump the statues.

Apollinaire found a different solution, and had the Iberian sculptures turned into a Parisian newspaper on September 6, accompanied by an anonymous note written by the "thief." But his plan went awry, and the police visited him the next day at his apartment at 37, rue Gros, where they found letters from Pieret. Convinced that the theft of the *Mona Lisa* was part of an international crime ring, they arrested Apollinaire for having sheltered Pieret, and the poet was thrown in prison (an experience he recorded in *Mes Prisons*). Apollinaire was released on September 13, but not before being grilled by the court. When asked why he did not reveal Pieret's statue theft earlier, he responded:

"Pieret is a little bit of my creation. He's very queer, very strange, and after studying him I made him into the hero of one of the last short stories in my *L'Hérésiarque et Cie.* So it would have been a kind of literary ingratitutde to let him starve," the poet responded.

In the end, it turned out that the *Mona Lisa* thief was not Pieret but an Italian housepainter who had wanted to restore the painting to its country of origin. It was recovered in 1913, but that did little to help Apollinaire, whose name was forever connected to the scandal.

Apollinaire's former residence
202, boulevard St.-Germain (7th arr.)
Métro: St.-Germain-des-Prés

In January 1913 Apollinaire left Auteuil for a top-floor room at 202, boulevard St.-Germain. His new home was just steps away from Les Deux Magots and Café Flore, where he and his *soirées de Paris* colleagues met to discuss future issues.

In 1918, shortly before his death, Apollinaire met and married Jacqueline Kolb. Their apartment was full of books, Cubist paintings, and African sculptures. André Breton later recalled spotting a painting from Picasso's blue period, "one or two beautiful Derains," and "two Chiricos which, even after consulting with the apartment's owner and with several others, I could never completely pull myself away from them . . . so greatly did they deepen the mental horizon."

Apollinaire's death in November 1918 came just two days before the Armistice was signed, and as he lay motionless on his bed, below his window the street filled with Parisians crying "Down with Guillaume!" The crowd was unaware of Apollinaire's death—they were referring to the Kaiser.

Apollinaire's wife stayed in the apartment until her death in 1967. Nearby is the rue Guillaume Apollinaire, named in 1951, on the thirty-third anniversary of his death.

Apollinaire statue

Square Laurent-Prache (6th arr.)
Métro: St.-Germain-des-Prés

In 1916, Apollinaire published *The Poet Assassinated*, two of whose characters included his former lover, the painter Marie Laurencin, and his friend Picasso.

Picasso's character is the "Benin bird"—named after the statue the painter was said to have in his studio—and is a barefoot, blue-shirted artist who lives in Montmartre. When his friend Croniamantal, "the best living poet," is assassinated, the Benin bird sculpts a strange memorial in his honor: it is little more than a hole—a statue of the void that the Benin bird says will hold the poet's ghost.

The real-life Picasso would sculpt a memorial for Apollinaire. Although the memorial was not the "void" statue described in *The Poet Assassinated*, the effect was no less surreal for those attending the dedication ceremony in 1959. When the covering was lifted in the square Laurent-Prache, onlookers gazed upon the bronze head not of Apollinaire but of a woman—Picasso's latest mistress and muse, Dora Maar.

The memorial stands in a small garden near the church of St.-Germain, not far from the rue Guillaume Apollinaire.

Henry Miller
(1891–1980)

It is now the fall of my second year in Paris. I was sent here for a reason I have not yet been able to fathom. I have no money, no resources, no hopes. I am the happiest man alive.

—Henry Miller
Tropic of Cancer, 1934

The vibrant expatriate life of Gertrude Stein and Ernest Hemingway and the decadent parties of F. Scott Fitzgerald had all but disappeared when Henry Miller arrived in Depression-era Paris in 1930. Prices were falling as unemployment climbed; many Americans had given up on Paris and returned home to the US. Le Dôme and La Coupole—cafés once known for their bohemians, rising talents, and wealthy expatriates—now catered to tourists and an eclectic mix of unpublished writers, second-rate artists, and eccentrics.

Miller felt at home among this crowd. He had arrived in Paris broke, and he stayed broke much of his time there. Although he found work at the Paris *Tribune*, the job did not last long—he preferred hanging around the American Express on 11, rue Scribe to see if money had been wired to him. At Le Dôme and La Coupole he often courted and entertained a tourist in the hopes of a free drink or a meal. And from his own friends he borrowed everything—from homes and hotel rooms to their overcoats and girlfriends. He spread out his borrowing, even devising a list to calculate how to eat dinner each day of the week at a different friend's home, exchanging his "charming" company for a free meal. During this time, he wrote his first story, which was inspired by a Parisian prostitute.

It did not take long for the backdrop of Paris and chaos of Miller's personal life to find their way into his first book, *Tropic of Cancer* (1934). The book's drama was provided by the disintegration of Miller's relationship with his wife, June. The catalyst was Miller's affair with Anaïs Nin, an aspiring French-born writer who would eventually become famous for her erotic diaries. Nin immediately impressed Henry with her wealth, exotic background, refined manners, and relentless self-analysis (when Miller met her she was on the forty-second volume of her diary). She became infatuated with both Henry and his wife, and soon the three were engaged in a destructive love triangle. June left Paris before Miller's book was finished, telling him: "And now you have your last chapter for your book."

With Nin supporting him financially, Henry's nomadic days came to an end, and he settled from 1932 to 1934 in an apartment with his friend Alfred Perlès on the rue de Clichy.

"Montmartre," Miller wrote in *Quiet Days in Clichy* (1940), "is worn, faded, derelict, nakedly vicious, mercenary, vulgar. It is, if anything, repellent rather than attractive, but insidiously repellent, like vice itself." But Miller was comfortable in this environment, and he wallpapered his room with book pages, marked with his favorite passages, and chain-smoked *Gaulouises bleues* as he typed furiously throughout the morning. In the afternoon, he changed into his wrinkled pajamas and took a nap, to be followed by a long walk or bike ride exploring the city. In *Tropic of Cancer*, he wrote:

> *The day opens in milky whiteness, streaks of salmon-pink sky, snails leaving their shells. Paris. Paris. Everything happens here. Old, crumbling walls and the pleasant sound of water running in the urinals. Men licking their mustaches at the bar. Shutters going up with a band and little streams purling in the gutter.*

Tropic of Cancer describes the story of a con artist, charmer, swindler, and womanizer at loose ends in the city as he writes his novel. Its frank depiction of sex and Paris's sleazier side was a departure from the refined language and romantic portrayal of Paris by F. Scott Fitzgerald, Edith Wharton, and other American writers who had preceded him:

> *Or wandering along the Seine at night, wandering and wandering, and going mad with the beauty of it, the trees leaning to, the broken images in the water . . . pushcarts stacked up like wine barrels in the side streets, the smell of berries in the market place, and the old church surrounded with vegetables and blue arc lights, the gutters slippery with garbage and women in satin pumps staggering through the filth and vermin at the end of an all-night souse.*

The book was published in Paris in September 1934 by the Englishman Jack Kahane, whose Obelisk Press specialized in obscene English-language books. It was sold at a special, low "smut" price, and soon stray copies were appearing in the US, where no publisher would dare print it. Most of Miller's peers gave enthusiastic reviews, although some did not know what to make of his plotless, raw style. Aldous Huxley, for example, praised the book but compared it to "certain kinds of folk music . . . which are pure unadulterated passion and engulf one completely in a way I can't stand for long."

The day *Tropic of Cancer* was published, Miller moved back to 18, villa Seurat, marking a new, successful period in his career. His friends often gathered there to listen to jazz or poetry readings. Miller would work through the racket, clanking away on his typewriter, a bottle of red wine on one side and pages of his new novel on the other.

Although Miller invoked Paris in later works such as *Quiet Days in Clichy* (1940), his time in the French capital ended with the onset of World War II and the publication of *Tropic of Capricorn*, a novel about his pre-Paris days of the 1920s.

Miller made sporadic trips to Paris with new wives (there would be five), and came on a final visit in 1969 for the filming of *Tropic of Cancer*. The book had finally seen publication in the US earlier that decade and had made Henry Miller a public name as well as an inspiration for a new generation of writers. The charming, penniless bohemian had become a wealthy man.

Sites

Hôtel St.-Germain-des-Prés

36, rue Bonaparte (6th arr.)
T: 01 43 26 00 19
www.hotel-paris-saint-germain.com
Métro: St.-Germain-des-Prés

Upon arriving in Paris in March of 1930, Miller moved into the Hôtel St.-Germain at 36, rue Bonaparte. Although he had few acquaintances in Paris, he was enchanted by the city:

> I love it here, I want to stay forever. . . . I will write here. I will live and write alone. And each day I will see a little more of Paris, study it, learn it as I would a book. . . . The streets sing, the stones talk. The houses drip history, glory, romance.

Miller enjoyed exploring his new neighborhood, which he later evoked in *Tropic of Cancer*:

> In the little garden adjoining the Église-St.-Germain-des-Prés are a few dismounted gargoyles. Monsters that jut forward with a terrifying plunge. On the benches other monsters—old people, idiots, cripples, epileptics. Snoozing there quietly, waiting for the dinner bell to ring.

Miller soon looked for housing elsewhere, working as a servant for an Indian pearl merchant and later an American lawyer. Both experiences inspired entertaining passages in *Tropic of Cancer*.

Villa Seurat

18, villa Seurat (14th arr.)
Métro: Alésia

"I am writing from the Villa Borghese. There's not a crumb of dirt anywhere, nor a chair misplaced. We are all alone here and we are dead," begins *Tropic of Cancer*.

The Villa Borghese of Miller's novel was in fact his home along the villa Seurat, a private cul-de-sac in the 14th arrondissement. Miller had first stayed there during his early years in Paris, when his nomad-like existence drew him to the home of his friend Michael Fraenkel. Previously occupied by the poet and playwright Antonin Artaud, Fraenkel's apartment had a skylight, a balcony, and a living room, one corner of which was Miller's designated spot.

The neighborhood around the villa Seurat was a rough, dirty section of Paris, where drunkards, prostitutes, and urchins loitered along the main street. But the villa Seurat was different—its brick houses were painted in shades of red, green, or pink, giving them, said Miller's friend Perlès, "a gingerbread quality." The apartments were large studios and had central heating—a huge step up from Miller's days of sleeping in cold hotel rooms or on office floors.

Miller returned to the villa Seurat in 1935, but this time the apartment was his own. For the next four years he stayed at no. 18, his primary residence as he wrote *Tropic of Capricorn*.

As Miller's fame as the author of *Tropic of Cancer* grew, so did the number of guests at his villa Seurat address: "The very mention of this street is sufficient to create longing and envy," he wrote. His crowd of admirers and friends included Perlès, Nin, and the author Lawrence Durrell, as well as a handful of others whom Perlès described as a bunch of "cranks, nuts, drunks, writers, artists, bums, Montparnasse derelicts, vagabonds, psychopaths . . . of all possible nationalities and sexes." Miller hung signs on his door—"If knock you must, knock after 11am," "*Je n'aime pas que l'on m'emmerde.*"—but the crowd came anyway, knowing he was in by the sound of his typewriter.

THE UNITED STATES OF AMERICA
PASSPORT

DEPARTMENT OF STATE

To all to whom these presents shall come, Greeting:

I, the undersigned, Secretary of State of the United States of America, hereby request all whom it may concern to permit

Janet Flanner

a citizen of the United States safely and freely to pass and in case of need to give *her* all lawful Aid and Protection

This passport is valid for use only in the following countries and for objects specified, unless amended

Greece Constantinople

France Italy

Private Life

Magazine Writer

The bearer is accompanied by _____

Given under my hand and the seal of the Department of State at the City of Washington, the *18th* day of *June* in the year *1921* and of the Independence of the United States the one hundred and forty-fifth.

Charles E. Hughes

PERSONAL DESCRIPTION

Age: 29 years
Height: 5 ft 3 in.
Forehead: medium
Eyes: blue
Nose: roman
Distinguishing marks:
Place of birth: Indianapolis, Ind.
Date of birth: March 13, 1891
Occupation: Writer

Mouth: medium
Chin: round
Hair: dark
Complexion: fair
Face:

Janet Flanner
SIGNATURE OF BEARER

No. 55504

Janet Flanner

(1892–1978)

The major scenic corners of the place St.-Germain-des-Prés are preserved immutably by their invaluable resistance to improvement. . . . Some of us passed fragments of our youth sitting out-of-doors on the broad, hospitable terrace of the Deux Magots café, facing the elderly church and its open garden of stunted trees.

—Janet Flanner, 1975

"I wanted beauty, with a capital B," explained Janet Flanner, recalling why she left New York in 1921 and headed to Europe. Before the decade was over, she would become known to readers of the *New Yorker* as Gênet, the Paris correspondent of the magazine that had made its debut in 1925.

For fifty years, Flanner sat in cluttered hotel rooms typing with two fingers the bimonthly letter from Gênet—a supposed Gallicized version of Janet's name. Flanner's first years in Paris were dominated by the vibrant Left Bank artist community, whose favorite spots and latest protégés she wrote about:

> *We had settled in the small hotels on the Paris Left Bank near the place St.-Germain-des-Prés, itself perfectly equipped with a large corner café called Les Deux Magots and an impressive twelfth-century Romanesque church, with its small garden of old trees, from whose branches the metropolitan blackbirds sang at dawn, audible to me in my bed close by in the rue Bonaparte. Though unacquainted with each other, as compatriots we soon discovered our chance similarity. We were a literary lot.*

Living in the Hôtel St.-Germain-des-Prés (the former home of Henry Miller and where Flanner would live for sixteen years), Flanner quickly became part of a community of expatriate women, including Gertrude Stein, Alice B. Toklas, Nancy Cunard, Nathalie Barney, and Sylvia Beach, the owner of the bookstore Shakespeare & Co., the "hearth and home of the Left Bank literary American colony." The bookstore was the first to publish James Joyce's *Ulysses* in 1922. Flanner, although not fond of Joyce himself, told the readers of the *New Yorker* that the sensation the book created on the Left Bank was "like an explosion in print whose words and phrases fell upon us like a gift of tongues, like a less than holy Pentecostal experience."

When the carefree days of the 1920s gave way to the Depression, and later the approaching political crisis in Europe, Flanner changed with the times, increasingly abandoning gossip for politics and contributing to the *New Yorker* as a general correspondent. If the Gênet of the 1920s had given *New Yorker* readers a vicarious taste of Parisian glamour, the Gênet of the 1930s and 1940s gave them a serious look at events unfolding in

Europe. What made her letters stand out among reports filed by other European correspondents were her details: in December 1940 she wrote of French children mocking German news broadcasts, of Parisians heading their letters to each other with "Paris, Germany," and of Parisians' unwavering character in the face of occupation —they still sat in the cafés, grumbling over politics, and were just as "logical, critical, disgusted, sardonic, witty, realistic, civilized as they always were."

Although she returned to the US in 1939, Flanner was back in Paris in late 1944, when she found the newly liberated city both eerie and broken-down. Her revived Paris letters became more opinionated—she criticized the Marshall Plan, for example, for subsidizing hotels over cultural institutions—but they also brought back the cheeky commentary *New Yorker* readers were used to from Gênet: writing about Café de Flore, which had risen to fame with the existentialists Jean-Paul Sartre and Simone de Beauvoir, she said, "The Café de

Henri Cartier-Bresson: *Janet Flanner, Paris, France,* 1958.

© Henri Cartier-Bresson/Magnum Photos

Flore serves as a drugstore for pretty upstate girls in unbecoming blue denim pants and their Middle Western dates, most of whom are growing hasty Beaux-Arts beards."

In fact, the more turbulent and modern Paris became during the 1960s, the more Flanner—now in her seventies—wished for the Paris of her youth. "As is natural in a highly civilized old city that has been enjoying solid prosperity, the architectural future of Paris is already crushing its past," she lamented in 1965. She hated the skyscrapers that were shooting up and the American slang that had crept into the French language, and she recalled the capital in the days when creativity and culture reigned. Even the Bois de Boulgone, once the "famous and fashionable pleasure garden," was now "passé in its romanticism," she claimed. And she feared the desertion of the medieval Les Halles food market near St.-Eustache could prompt an end to French cuisine. Flanner tried to turn toward the lighter side of Parisian life—the public's reaction to the latest Jean-Luc Godard film, Maria Callas at the Opéra, or Brigitte Bardot's topless New Year's TV special—but the reality of this new Paris weighed on her.

Yet in her final Paris letter, written in 1975, Flanner admitted that much of Paris still looked like it did when she had first arrived in the 1920s: "In most respects it has not changed an iota. Old cities are monuments to themselves, not easily altered, and with difficulty even repaired."

Sites

Hôtel Continental (Hotel InterContinental)

2, rue Scribe (1st arr.)
Tel: 01 40 07 32 32
www.paris-ic.intercontinental.com
Métro: Tuileries

In the fall of 1949, Flanner moved with her companion, Solita Solano, to the Hôtel Continental, a Second Empire building whose site was originally a seventeenth-century Capuchin monastery. In her small, cluttered room, surrounded by manuscripts, newspapers, and articles, she managed to fit in some furniture, including a bed, buffet, and wood chiffonier whose missing bottom drawers she filled with books.

There, she followed a routine she had established in her Hôtel St.-Germain days of the 1920s and 1930s, shutting herself up in the hotel for a day or two, cigarette smoke filling her room as she agonized over the composition of her next Paris letter. Her balcony offered a respite from work and provided a view of the Tuileries. (During the fight for Algerian independence, Flanner could hear bombs exploding on nearby avenues.)

In 1954, the *New Yorker* published Flanner's two-part profile of André Malraux, a writer, former Resistance leader, and at the time de Gaulle's minister of information. It had been one of her most exhausting projects, as the research she turned up on the enigmatic Malraux had been extensive and overwhelming. Finding little that provided true insight into his character, she turned to the staff of the Hôtel Continental to collect whatever gossip or anecdotes they could offer her about the famous Frenchman: one of the waiters gave her a postcard of a château where his brother had hid Malraux and lent the writer money during the war.

The hotel staff liked Flanner, who made the hotel bar a second home. One of her visitors, *New Yorker* editor Gardner Botsford, recalled spotting Flanner there:

> . . . sitting in a great big leather arm-chair at the end of the room, say, about four o'clock in the afternoon, and then all these people, every nationality, would be sitting on little funeral chairs in a line, and one could go up and talk to Janet, and every-body would move up one chair. And

> Janet knew them all, dealt with all their problems, promised to read their manuscripts, told them if their last piece was either good or no good.

Although Flanner would live in the hotel for roughly two decades, near the end of her life she moved to the elegant Ritz, which was more befitting of her stature as an award-winning *New Yorker* writer. But she balked at the price of her new dwellings, and was soon back at the Continental, only to find that its renovated, modern look displeased her. She headed back to the Ritz.

Les Deux Magots

6, place St.-Germain-des-Prés (6th arr.)
T: 01 45 48 55 25
www.lesdeuxmagots.fr
Métro: Saint-Germain-des-Prés

When Solita Solano arrived with Janet Flanner in Paris from America in the 1920s, she discovered that some of the most appealing St.-Germain cafés —namely Les Deux Magots and the Café Flore—were "rapidly filling with the accents we hoped to leave behind."

Nevertheless, she and Flanner liked to begin their day with breakfast at Les Deux Magots, which they found to be a more sophisticated alternative to the rowdy Montparnasse expatriate cafés that their friend Ernest Hemingway went to, such as La Rotonde and Le Dôme.

Les Deux Magots drew a group of Surrealists, who Flanner later recalled in the introduction to her collection of 1925–1939 Paris letters, *Paris Was Yesterday*:

> The Surrealists had their own club table facing the door of the Deux Magots, from which vantage point a seated Surrealist could conveniently insult any newcomer with whom he happened to be feuding, or discuss his plan to horsewhip an editor of some belligerent anti-Surrealist newspaper for having mentioned his name or, worse, for having failed to mention it.

Flanner and Hemingway—friends since the 1920s—had their special table at Les Deux Magots, located at the back of the café.

Private collection.

F. Scott Fitzgerald

(1896–1940)

He wanted to see the blue hour spread
over the magnificent façade, and imagine
that the cab horns, playing endlessly the
first few bars of Le Plus que Lent, *were*
the trumpets of the Second Empire.

—F. Scott Fitgerald
"The Swimmers," 1929

F. Scott Fitzgerald, Zelda, and Scottie in Paris.

When F. Scott Fitzgerald arrived in Paris in 1925, he had already written *This Side of Paradise* and *The Great Gatsby*, and was known for his wild and luxurious lifestyle. He and his wife, Zelda, were looking to "find a new rhythm" for their lives, and Paris, with its vibrant artistic scene and low cost of living, was an attractive option for many Americans. "France has the only two good things toward which we drift as we grow older—intelligence and good manners," said Scott, although he and Zelda—both heavy drinkers—often exhibited little of the latter.

The Fitzgeralds moved to Paris in the spring, settling on the Right Bank at 14, rue de Tilsitt near the Arc de Triomphe. But the Paris where the Fitzgeralds spent most of their time and that would appear in Scott's work, was the 6th arrondissement, the quarter of the Luxembourg Gardens, galleries and cafés, wealthy Americans, and writers. Fitzgerald, then twenty-eight, was soon writing home to the author H.L. Mencken that he had "met most of the American literary world here (the crowd that centers about [Ezra] Pound) and find them mostly junk-dealers; except a few like

Hemingway who are doing rather more thinking and working."

Fitzgerald published several works between 1920 and 1926, but the sales from *The Great Gatsby* (1925) were not up to expectations, and he was forced to turn to writing commercial short stories for American magazines to support his lavish lifestyle, which included cocktails at the Ritz and lunch on the Champs-Élysées. When he could, he worked on a new novel, *Tender Is the Night*, but he could always be lured away from his desk to a jazz club in Montmartre or a party on the Left Bank. It was a time of "1000 parties and no work," he later recalled.

After a brief stay in the US, Scott and Zelda returned to Paris in 1928 brimming with new plans: Scott hoped to devote more time to his novel, while Zelda, who had recently taken up dancing, wished to become a ballerina. Their new apartment was at 58, rue de Vaugirard, close to the Luxembourg Gardens. It would be this same address, "high above the green mass of leaves," that would become the model for the Paris home of Dick and Nicole Diver in *Tender Is the Night*. The apartment was also just around the corner from Gertrude Stein (then on the rue de Fleurus), whom Fitzgerald had met through Hemingway a few years earlier and who had become a great supporter of his work. Zelda, however, was less impressed with Gertrude and found her full of "sententious gibberish." Nor was she pleased by her husband's close relationship with Ernest Hemingway, whom she found boorish.

By 1929, Fitzgerald's alcoholism consumed him. In the largely autobiographical *Tender Is the Night*, he wrote: "The drink made past happy things contemporary with the present, as if they were still going on, contemporary even with the future as if they were about to happen again."

As his drunken antics grew worse and Zelda became more fanatical about becoming a dancer, the couple's erratic behavior alienated friends. The "snub list" that Fitzgerald had once jokingly created grew longer, as even his friends began to distance themselves. He turned up drunk to have tea with Edith Wharton; James Joyce, after meeting him, declared, "He'll do himself an injury some day." Fitzgerald was not oblivious to the bridges he had burned, and in his story "Babylon Revisited," about an alcoholic father

returning to Paris during the Depression to see his daughter, he wrote:

I spoiled this city for myself. I didn't realize it, but the days came along one after another, and then two years were gone, and everything was gone, and I was gone.

By 1930, the promises of Europe and the "new rhythm" he and Zelda had searched for had vanished. They had spent the previous summer on the Riviera, where Zelda had tried to drive her car off a cliff. Back in Paris that fall, they moved to 10, rue Pergolèse off the avenue de la Grande Armée. Within six months of their return, Zelda had a breakdown and entered a hospital. The Fitzgeralds decided to leave France for a clinic in Switzerland.

"Switzerland is a country where very few things begin, but many things end," wrote Fitzgerald in his story "One Trip Abroad." And in fact, the writer would revisit Paris only in his prose. Paris was the setting for three of his later short stories, "The Bridal Party," "News of Paris, Fifteen Years Ago," and "Babylon Revisited." It would also have a prominent role in several other works, notably in *Tender Is the Night*, which was finally pub-

lished in 1934. Between 1924 and 1934, Fitzgerald drafted seven different versions of the novel, in which Paris is invoked in a romantic, nostalgic haze:

…and lovers now they fell ravenously on the quick seconds while outside the taxi windows the green and cream twilight faded, and the fire-red, gas-blue, ghost-green signs begin to shine smokily through the tranquil rain. It was nearly six, the streets were in movement, the bistros gleamed, the Place de la Concorde moved by in pink majesty as the cab turned north.

Sites

Harry's New York Bar

5, rue Daunou (2nd arr.)
T: 01 42 61 71 14
Métro: Opéra

The sign on the wall reads "Sank Roo Doe Noo"—an aid for the bar's non-French-speaking customers struggling to pronounce the bar's address to taxi drivers. Fitzgerald, who once summed up his French by saying "Je suis a stranger here," made little attempt to learn the language or mix with the locals, preferring his wealthy American friends.

Harry's New York Bar was a favorite of Fitzgerald, a Princeton graduate, who could look above and see college banners and other Americana on the bar's dark wood paneling. The bar was the birthplace of the Sidecar and the Bloody Mary and then, as now, primarily drew Americans. Hemingway could also often be spotted there, typically following a few rounds of sparring at the Montmartre Sportif.

Prunier Restaurant (Goumard)

9, rue Duphot (1st arr.)
T: 01 42 60 36 07
www.goumard.com
Métro: Concord or Madeleine

Fitzgerald and Hemingway met shortly after Fitzgerald's arrival in Paris. *The Great Gatsby* had been published just two weeks earlier, and the contrast between the two authors was striking: Fitzgerald was an established novelist; Hemingway was still writing short stories for small magazines. Despite Fitzgerald's success, he was enamored with Hemingway's style and personality—going so far as to model the medieval knight of his "Count of Darkness" stories on the other writer. He did his best to promote Hemingway's work, reading and editing *The Sun Also Rises* (1926) and helping Hemingway land an important book contract with Scribner's. Hemingway would later repay Fitzgerald by portraying him as a drunk, irresponsible cuckold who had betrayed his talent to make quick money writing mediocre stories.

Founded in 1872, Prunier was an elegant seafood restaurant near the place de la Madeleine. The restaurant was out of Hemingway's budget for most of the 1920s, but not that of the Fitzgeralds, who favored Emile Prunier's bouillabaisse.

In June of 1929, Fitzgerald was having lunch here with Hemingway and one of his boxing buddies, the Canadian writer Morley Callaghan. Hemingway and Callaghan decided to box a round, with Fitzgerald as the timekeeper.

The match took place after lunch. Callaghan's fist connected with Hemingway's lip, and Hemingway spit a mouthful of blood at Callaghan. Fitzgerald was so transfixed that he forgot to keep time and let the round extend past the one-minute period agreed upon. When Callaghan knocked Hemingway down, Hemingway accused Fitzgerald of letting the time pass out of jealousy. In the version he later told friends, it was some pre-match drinks—and not Callaghan's superior boxing skills—that had determined the outcome.

The seafood restaurant is open today and has preserved its original oak woodwork and 1930s etched glass.

Site of Bricktop's

1, rue Fontaine (9th arr.)
Métro: Blanche or Pigalle

> After an hour he left and strolled
> toward Montmartre, up the Rue
> Pigalle into the Place Blanche. He
> passed a lighted door from which
> issued music, and stopped with the
> sense of familiarity; it was Bricktop's,
> where he had parted with so many
> hours and so much money.

The Montmartre nightclub that Fitzgerald evoked in his 1931 story, "Babylon Revisited," was one of the most influential jazz clubs of 1920s and 1930s Paris. It was owned by the red-haired African-American performer Bricktop, and it drew musicians such as Sidney Bechet, Stéphane Grapelli, and Django Reinhardt. Fitzgerald had discovered the place in 1925 and soon joined Bricktop's group of fans, including Cole Porter and later the Duke and Duchess of Windsor—who flocked to the club to watch Bricktop dance the Charleston, which was then sweeping Paris.

As one of Fitzgerald's friends, Bricktop was called upon more than once to save the writer, whom she called a "little boy in a man's body." Once, she appeased police who had brought him to her club after catching him playing in the fountain at the Lido cabaret; another time she had to calm a cab driver upset that a drunken Fitzgerald had kicked his windows in. It was a rare night, she said, that she did not escort him home.

By the time Fitzgerald wrote "Babylon Revisited" he had left Paris and adopted a more somber perspective. The story's protagonist returns to Paris only to discover that he no longer feels at home. The familiar faces of the Ritz have disappeared, and the loud music and lights of Montmartre seem foreign: "So much for the effort and ingenuity of Montmartre. All the catering to vice and waste was on an utterly childish scale," he says, before turning away from the bustling quarter.

Carl Van Vechten: *Bricktop*, June 22, 1934.
Library of Congress Prints and Photographs Division, Washington, D.C.

BOOKSHOP

Ernest Hemingway

(1899–1961)

If you were lucky enough to have lived in Paris as a young man, then wherever you go for the rest of your life, it stays with you, for Paris is a moveable feast.

—Ernest Hemingway
A Moveable Feast, 1964

Ernest Hemingway and Sylvia Beach in front of Shakespeare & Co., Paris.

Ernest Hemingway arrived in Paris in December 1921, a young reporter for the *Toronto Star* on assignment to write about the French capital. It was not his first time in Europe: the Illinois-born writer had driven an ambulance for the Red Cross in Italy during World War I.

He and his wife, Hadley, first stopped in St.-Germain at the Hôtel Jacob et d'Angleterre (still at 44, rue Jacob), then an affordable haven for Americans. It was where, in the eighteenth century, the British met with Benjamin Franklin, John Adams, and John Jay to negotiate a treaty for US independence.

The Hemingways then rented an apartment nearby in the Latin Quarter, avoiding the expatriate hub of Montparnasse in favor of the working-class area of the place de la Contrescarpe. Located near what Hemingway called the "cesspool of the rue Mouffetard," the apartment at 74, rue du Cardinal-Lemoine was a fourth-floor walk-up whose "enameled crater in the floor" was "not uncomfortable to anyone who has used a Michigan outhouse." Around the corner, past narrow, hilly streets, was Hemingway's studio at 39, rue Descartes, the same address where the poet Paul Verlaine had died twenty-five years earlier. "There was never another part of Paris that he loved like that," Hemingway wrote in "The Snows of Kilimanjaro."

The writer's first days in Paris were largely devoted to writing articles for the *Toronto Star*. He wrote about the French and their culture—all without speaking to the people or knowing any French.

It was not until 1924, following trips to Spain and North America, that Hemingway found the inspiration he had been seeking. His first novel, *The Sun Also Rises*, his classic tale about bullfighting set in France and Spain, was published in 1926.

His new productivity coincided with increased involvement in Paris's expatriate literary scene. The same Hemingway who in 1921 had avoided joining the literati in Montparnasse three years later was renting an apartment in that very area. He and Hadley lived with their newborn son, John, at 113, rue Notre-Dame-des-Champs (the building no longer stands). The apartment was located above a sawmill and lacked electricity, but Hemingway did not mind. The energy of Montparnasse—its cafés and cabarets—

made the place seem promising. "The tables are full—they are always full—someone is moved down and crowded together, something is knocked over, more people come in at the swinging door," he wrote.

La Closerie des Lilas and Le Dôme ranked among his favorites, but there was also the Dingo Bar (then at 10, rue Delambre), where he first met F. Scott Fitzgerald, and Le Falstaff (42, rue du Montparnasse), which still serves English food and drinks. Brasserie Lipp (151, boulevard St.-Germain) was good for beer and Alsatian food, and Les Deux-Magots for a *café crème* with James Joyce.

Hemingway initially disdained any café associated with bohemia. He claimed that Café de la Rotonde (105, boulevard du Montparnasse) was where the "scum of Greenwich Village, New York, has been skimmed off and deposited in large ladles." The Sélect (99, boulevard du Montparnasse) was nothing but a "collection of inmates." And Le Trou dans le Mur (The Hole in the Wall, then at 23, boulevard des Capucines) was "a hangout for deserters and for dope peddlers during and after the first war."

Café tables often served as his writing desk, and occasionally are featured in his works. The Café de la Paix (still at 5, place de l'Opéra) was the backdrop for his short story "My Old Man," while the Dingo Bar set the stage for "A Sea Change." And in *The Sun Also Rises*, the character Jake claims, "No matter what café in Montparnasse you ask a taxi driver to bring you to from the right bank of the river, they always take you to the Rotonde."

By the late 1920s, Hemingway's Paris years were coming to a close. His infidelity had ended his marriage to Hadley; by 1927 he lived with his second wife, Pauline Pfeiffer, at 6, rue Férou, near the St.-Sulpice church. "I have a theory that Ernest needs a new woman for each big book," said his friend F. Scott Fitzgerald.

Seven years after his arrival as a poor journalist, Hemingway left Paris as a successful writer. He returned to Paris, but only as a visitor. Paris, he said in the 1930s, "was a fine place to be quite young in and . . . a necessary part of a man's education. . . . But she is like a mistress who does not grow old and she has other lovers now."

Sites

La Closerie des Lilas

171, boulevard du Montparnasse (14th arr.)
T: 01 40 51 34 50
Métro: Port-Royal

> The Closerie des Lilas was the nearest good café when we lived in the flat over the sawmill at 113 rue Notre-Dame-des-Champs, and it was one of the best cafés in Paris. It was warm inside in the winter and in the spring and fall it was very fine outside with the table under the shade of the trees on the side where the statue of Marshal Ney was, and the square, regular tables under the big awnings along the boulevard.
> — *A Moveable Feast*, 1964

One of several expatriate cafés along the boulevard du Montparnasse, La Closerie des Lilas was one of Hemingway's favorites and where he did much of his early-morning writing. Hemingway was particularly fond of the terrace, where he could gaze upon one of Napoleon's men, Marshal Ney, and "keep the statue company."

Hemingway wrote his short story "Big Two-Hearted River" "with the afternoon light coming in over [his]

shoulder," and rewrote sections of *The Sun Also Rises*. The book's protagonists also appreciated La Closerie des Lilas, where they went to drink whiskeys and soda. "One's an ass to leave Paris," declares his character Brett, as she sits on the café terrace.

Today a plaque commemorates the café's former patron, and one can still sit and gaze at the distinguished Marshal Ney.

Le Café du Dôme

108, boulevard du Montparnasse (14th arr.)
T: 01 43 35 34 82
Métro: Vavin

While many of his literary acquaintances could be spotted at La Rotonde or Le Sélect, Hemingway preferred to cross the street to Le Dôme, where, he said, "there were people . . . who worked."

Although it is now a restaurant, in Hemingway's day the Dôme was an enclosed café filled with ordinary Parisians. Like the characters in his short story "Mr. and Mrs. Elliot," Hemingway sat in Le Dôme, "avoiding the Rotonde across the street because it is always so full of foreigners."

Le Dôme was one of Hemingway's first discoveries upon arriving in Paris, and in the winter of 1921, when few Parisians could be spotted on a café terrace, he and Hadley sat outside and took in their new city:

> We sit outside the Dome Café, opposite the Rotonde that's being redecorated, warmed up against one of those charcoal braziers and it's so damned cold outside and the brazier makes it so warm and we drink rum punch, hot, and the rum enters in to us like the Holy Spirit.

Hemingway Bar, Hôtel Ritz

15, place Vendôme (1st arr.)
T: 01 43 16 33 63
Métro: Tuileries

World War II was drawing to a close when the owner of Shakespeare & Co., Sylvia Beach, looked out her window and saw Ernest Hemingway traveling down the rue de l'Odéon, followed by a string of jeeps.

> [Hemingway] was in battle dress, grimy and bloody. A machine gun clanked on the floor. . . . He wanted to know if there was anything he could do for us. We asked him if he could do something about the Nazi snipers on the rooftops in our street, particularly on Adrienne's rooftop. He got his company out of the jeeps and took them up to the roof. We heard firing for the last time in the rue de l'Odéon. Hemingway and his men came down again and rode off in their jeeps—"to liberate," according to Hemingway "the cellar at the Ritz." He led several soldiers through the place Vendôme and into the chic hotel, where he proceeded to order seventy-three dry martinis.

Years later, the Ritz renamed the smaller of its two bars in his honor. The Hemingway Bar, which is at the end of the right-hand corridor as you enter the Ritz, is today one of the coziest and priciest bars in Paris. Celebrities and wealthy foreigners are often spotted in its small, wood-paneled room, where the *cognac aux truffes* (cognac with truffles) costs about the same as a meal in an average French bistro. The bar previously had its entrance at 38, rue Cambon, but the Ritz nowadays prefers its bar guests to enter through their main entrance off the place Vendôme—past the scrutinizing gaze of its doorman.

Henry Strater: *First portrait of Ernest Hemingway*.
Ogunquit Museum of American Art, Ogunquit, Maine.

NATIONAL UNION OF JOURNALISTS

7 John Street, Bedford Row, London, W.C.1

'Phone :
HOLborn 2258

Telegrams :
Natujay Holb, London

This is to certify that

Mr. GEORGE ORWELL

of The Tribune

is a member of the......... T.-&.P.
Branch of the National Union of Journalists.

Leslie R. Algous Branch Sec.

(Address) 66. Priory Gdns.. N.6.

.... Member's Sig.

George Orwell

(1903–1950)

Paris is vulgar—half grandiosity and
half slums.

—George Orwell
Down and Out in Paris and London, 1933

Five years with the Indian Imperial Police in colonial Burma changed the life of young, middle-class Englishman George Orwell (Eric Blair). Having witnessed and participated in the colonial exploitation of Burmese natives, Orwell returned to England in his early twenties determined never again to play a part in such "evil despotism."

He announced his intention to become a writer and was soon packing his bags for the City of Light, his vision of which consisted of "sitting in cafés with foreign art students, drinking white wine and talking about Marcel Proust."

When Orwell arrived in Paris in the spring of 1928 at the age of twenty-four, the successful years of *Animal Farm* (1945) and *1984* (1949) were far off. He took up residence at 6, rue du Pot-de-Fer in the 5th arrondissement, close to the Panthéon and the Sorbonne. He visited popular cafés like Les Deux Magots and Le Dôme, but for the most part he avoided Paris's expatriate and literary scenes, preferring to mix with locals in the bistros and bars of his neighborhood. While Hemingway and Fitzgerald put Montparnasse on the map for Americans, Orwell found the influx of American tourists and aspiring artists distasteful:

> *During the boom years . . . Paris was invaded by such a swarm of artists, writers, students, dilettanti, sight-seers, debauchers and plain idlers as the world has probably never seen. In some quarters of the town the so-called artists must actually have outnumbered the working population—indeed, it has been reckoned that in the late twenties there were as many as 30,000 painters in Paris, most of them imposters. The populace has grown so hardened to artists that gruff-voiced Lesbians in corduroy breeches and young men in Grecian or medieval costume could walk the streets without attracting a glance, and along the Seine banks by Notre Dame it was almost impossible to pick one's way between the sketching-stools. It was the age of dark horses and neglected genii; the phrase on everybody's lips was "Quand je serai lancé."*

But Orwell was among the many hoping to launch their writing careers in Paris. Few were interested in the short stories he produced, however,

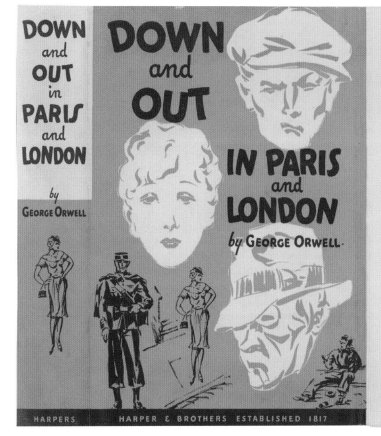

DOWN
and
OUT
in
PARIS
and
LONDON

by
GEORGE ORWELL

DOWN
and
OUT
IN PARIS
and
LONDON
by GEORGE ORWELL

HARPERS   HARPER & BROTHERS ESTABLISHED 1817

What the English Critics Say about
DOWN AND OUT
IN PARIS AND LONDON
by George Orwell

J. B. Priestley: "Uncommonly good reading. An excellent book and a valuable social document."

Compton Mackenzie: "A clearly genuine human document, which at the same time is written with so much simple force that in spite of the squalor and degradation thus unfolded, the result is curiously beautiful with the beauty of an accomplished etching on copper."

Time and Tide: "My advice to those who can afford it is: buy this book. If you cannot run to purchase, get it from the library. By one means or other, read it."

Times Literary Supplement: "A vivid picture of an apparently mad world."

The New Leader: "It is a magnificent book, courageously done, and without bravado or self pity. A terrible indictment of existing conditions."

Sunday Express: "A terrible, fascinating, and necessary-to-be-read account of utter destitution, illumined by hope and determination."

HARPER & BROTHERS, Publishers

No. 2414

and when his income as an English teacher dried up, Orwell found himself broke. He had money back in England, but he decided to stick it out in Paris. The result of his experience was *Down and Out in Paris and London*.

With no income, Orwell spent much of his time in bed, warding off hunger and boredom in his room along the rue du Pot-de-Fer (the fictionalized rue Coq d'Or). His hotel was inhabited by workmen, students, prostitutes, and the occasional thief. There was an old couple who sold fake pornographic photos on the boulevard St.-Michel, and an Englishman who spent half of each year drunk in France. Orwell wove their stories—and those of the various figures he met during his tramping—into his Paris narrative.

When hunger became unbearable, Orwell attempted to obtain a workman's job, but his lack of experience—and in particular his smooth hands—betrayed his bourgeois background. He also tried fishing in the Seine to little success: "The Seine is full of dace, but they grew cunning during the siege of Paris, and none of them

has been caught since, except in nets."

He finally found work as a *plongeur*—a dishwasher, or "a slave's slave." As he worked long hours to make ends meet, he observed the wide divide between the lives of the workers and those on the receiving end of their services.

He took several humorous jabs at Parisian life. Pawnshops, he said, should be visited in the afternoon: "The clerks are French, and, like most French people, are in a bad temper till they have eaten their lunch." He also claimed that "the surest sign of a bad restaurant is to be frequented only by foreigners" and that "the more one pays for food, the more sweat and spittle one is obliged to eat with it," as the best, most exacting French cooks and waiters are constantly dipping their fingers into dishes to ensure the quality of a dish.

Having earned little more than twenty pounds during the first year of his writing career, Orwell left Paris in December 1929 for England. His stay in Paris had lasted only one-and-a-half years, and yet the memories of Parisian poverty had a lasting effect on him. His exposure to the realities of poverty resulted in a critical examination of society, class, and institutions.

A few years later, en route to fight in the Spanish Civil War, he stopped in Paris to see the American author Henry Miller. In the cab on the way to Miller's home, Orwell got into a fight with his driver over a three-franc fare and the two nearly came to blows. Afterward, he realized the reason behind the driver's aggressiveness:

With my English accent I had appeared to him as a symbol of the idle, patronizing foreign tourists who had done their best to turn France into something midway between a museum and a brothel. In his eyes an English tourist meant a bourgeois. He was getting a bit of his own back on the parasites who were normally his employers. And it struck me that the motives of the polyglot army that filled the train, and of the peasants with raised fists out there in the fields, and my own motive in going to Spain, and the motive of the old taxi-driver in insulting me, were at bottom all the same.

Sites

Rue du Pot-de-Fer

(5th arr.)
Métro: Mabillon

> The rue du Coq d'Or, Paris, seven in the morning. A succession of furious, choking yells from the street. Madame Monce, who kept the little hotel opposite mine, had come out on to the pavement to address a lodger on the third floor. Her bare feet were stuck into sabots and her grey hair was streaming down.
>
> MADAME MONCE: '*Salope*! *Salope*! How many times have I told you not to squash bugs on the wallpaper? Do you think you've bought the hotel, eh? Why can't you throw them out of the window like everyone else? *Putain! Salope*!'

Shortly after arriving in Paris, George Orwell moved into a cheap hotel at 6, rue du Pot-de-Fer, the street whose hodgepodge of eccentric, poor residents he would make famous in *Down and Out in Paris and London*. In Orwell's story, the rue du Pot de Fer becomes the rue du Coq d'Or, home to the Hôtel des Trois Moineaux.

"It was a very narrow street—a ravine of tall, leprous houses, lurching towards one another in queer attitudes, as though they had all been frozen in the act of collapse," he wrote. He called it a representative Paris slum, made up of workers, prosititutes, and tramps, and bugs that "marched all day like columns of soldiers."

As in much of the rest of the 5th arrondissement, today's high rent along the rue du Pot-de-Fer has pushed out the workers and tramps of Orwell's time and replaced them with restaurants and art shops.

Hôtel Lotti

7, rue Castiglione (1st arr.)
T: 01 42 60 60 62
Métro: Tuileries
www.jollyhotels.com

One of the many odd jobs Orwell attempted while in Paris was as a dishwasher at the Hôtel Lotti, a luxury hotel off the rue de Rivoli.

Orwell quickly learned that as a dishwasher he occupied the lowest rank in the kitchen workers' elaborate caste system, which consisted of foul-mouthed cooks, snobby waiters, and hardworking *plongeurs*—whose long work days were filled with quarreling and mealtime mayhem. Orwell, however, was most taken by the contrast between the kitchen and the world outside, where American tourists dined on overpriced food.

> It was amusing to look round the filthy little scullery and think that only a double door was between us and the dining-room. There sat the customers in all their splendour—spotless table-cloths, bowls of flowers, mirrors and gilt cornices and painted cherubim; and here, just a few feet away, we in our disgusting filth. For it really was disgusting filth.

The Hôtel Lotti, which served as the inspiration for "Hotel X" in *Down and Out in Paris and London*, has recently undergone extensive renovation.

Former residence of Nellie Limouzin

14, avenue de Corbera (12th arr.)
Métro: Reuilly-Diderot or Diderot

"In France everyone can remember a certain amount of civil disturbance, and even the workmen in the bistros talk of *la révolution*—meaning the next revolution, not the last one," wrote Orwell in 1932.

Paris not only opened Orwell's eyes to the life of the poor, it also was the site of his political education. As the 1930s approached, France's political climate was once again unstable: as Facism began to rise in Italy and Nazism in Germany, conservatives regained power in France. Shortly before Orwell's arrival in spring 1928, Communists were arrested under suspicion of plotting to overthrow the state.

Orwell's aunt Nellie Limouzin, and her lover, the Esperanto language activist Eugëne Adam, welcomed Orwell into their home, from which they ran an Esperantist workers' association. The left-leaning couple engaged Orwell in spirited political debate, and Orwell later pointed to his time in Paris as influential in forming his identity as a socialist. Some scholars also believe that some of the Newspeak language Orwell created in *1984* can be traced back to his exposure to Esperanto in Paris.

Georges Simenon

(1903–1989)

It was November. Dusk was falling. From his office window he could see a stretch of the Seine, the Place Saint-Michel, and a floating wash-house, all shrouded in a blue haze through which the gas lamps twinkled like stars as they lit up one by one.

—Georges Simenon
The Strange Case of Peter the Lett, 1931

Georges Simenon (second from left), Josephine Baker, and friends.

The opening lines of *The Strange Case of Peter the Lett* (1931) describe a view familiar to thousands of readers around the world who know 36, quai des Orfèvres as the police headquarters of the fictional Inspector Jules Maigret.

By the age of twenty-eight, Belgian-born Georges Simenon had already published 190 pulp novels under seventeen pseudonyms. But it was not until he invented Inspector Maigret in 1931 that he was transformed from a modestly successful author to a best-selling one, his books reputedly becoming the most frequently stolen from Parisian libraries.

At a time when France was looking to escape the memories of World War I, and later World War II, the humdrum Paris of Inspector Maigret—who liked beer and the cinema—offered a comforting escape. Maigret's Paris was the Paris of ordinary Parisians, where one could smell roasting coffee coming from the Balthazar shop along the avenue de l'Opéra or watch the slow shuffle of the store-owners in the quiet place St.-Sulpice. A Paris where the most quotidian scenes—the "soiled tablecloth, coffee cups, glasses of brandy or liquor" of a bistro—filled readers with a sense of familiarity.

Aside from his headquarters on the quai des Orfèvres and his home at 132, boulevard Richard-Lenoir, Maigret's Paris was often that of the seediest quarters, places of gangsters and prostitutes, of "sordid, leering figures" and "furnished hotels with front doors discreetly ajar."

Parisian streets provided more than just a location for a murder or a robbery—they were key to identifying the nature of the crime or the character of the victim or witness. Readers knew, for example, that when Maigret entered the rue de la Roquette, near the Bastille, he was looking for a rough, lower-class criminal, not a white-collar murderer from the 16th arrondissement.

Maigret grew so popular that in 1934 Simenon was asked to take on the real-life case of the mysterious death of a court magistrate. Readers devoured his *Paris-Soir* newspaper articles, in which he concluded that the mafia was behind the crime. When the police finally proved that the magistrate had committed suicide, the public could hardly believe that Maigret had failed them.

Despite the embarrassment of the *Paris-Soir* incident, Simenon's novels continued to sell well. The writer who had arrived poor in Paris in 1922 was by middle age a slightly plump, bourgeois man who dined at Maxim's (3, rue Royale), dressed in sleek suits and fedoras, drove a large green sports car, and had left the Marais for an upscale neighborhood outside of the city.

Unlike many French writers, he did not find his comfortable lifestyle greatly disturbed by World War II. He had moved to France's Vendée region in 1940, and as a foreigner he was banned from leaving the region to travel to Paris. The captivity distressed Simenon, but he soon made connections with Occupation officials who granted him passes to visit Paris (and his favorite brothels).

In 1945, Simenon decided to leave for the US, where he would live for a decade. He felt the American way of life was more akin to his own. He had never fit in with the Parisian literati—he sang in the revered halls of his publisher Gallimard and walked out of a meeting of the prestigious *Société des Gens de Lettres* (Society of Men of Letters). He preferred William Faulkner and Ernest Hemingway to French writers; his favorite music was Dixieland jazz. English even began to creep into his novels, although the setting was still often France.

He returned to Europe for a promotional tour in 1952, and a few years later would make a definitive return, avoiding the energy and glamour of Paris for a quieter existence in Switzerland. But that year, at the age of forty-nine, Simenon basked in the attention that greeted him when he arrived in the French capital. Among the several parties held in his honor, his favorite was that given at 36, quai des Orfèvres, where the Parisian judiciary presented him with a special badge, no. 0000, issued in his honor.

George Simenon in front of 36, quai d'Orfèvres.

Sites

Simenon's former residence
21, place des Vosges (4th arr.)
Métro: Chemin-Vert, St.-Paul, Bastille.

"When I came to Paris, and was very poor, I remember living on just a herring a day. I understood that I was not ready to write true novels, but had to make my apprenticeship," Simenon recalled near the end of his life.

He had arrived in Paris in 1922, determined to avoid the typical artist's poverty and obscurity. He first stayed in the home of a friend, then worked his way through a series of small quarters before moving in 1923 to a ground–floor apartment on the place des Vosges—once the home to Victor Hugo, Madame de Sévigné, and other eminent figures of Paris's literary past. He later acquired an additional apartment on the third floor, which he decorated in an Art Deco style he believed reminiscent of an American diner.

Although Simenon's own apartment at no. 21 had once belonged to the Duke de Richelieu, the Marais of the 1920s no longer enjoyed its former prestige as a home of the bourgeois or nobility. Its resident craftsmen and tailors provided little in the way of exotic nightlife, and Simenon and his wife, Tigy, instead crossed the river to Montparnasse, where they frequented La Rotonde, Le Dôme, and La Coupole with the likes of Pablo Picasso, Max Jacob, and André Derain. Simenon also left his home in the Marais to drop in on his favorite brothels, including the Sphinx (at 31, boulevard Edgar-Quinet, immortalized in Henry Miller's *Tropic of Cancer*) and Madame Hélène's at 26, rue Brey.

Théâtre des Champs-Élysées

15, avenue Montaigne (8th arr.)
T: 01 49 52 50 50
www.theatrechampselysees.fr
Métro: Alma-Marceau or Franklin-Roosevelt

In October 1925, *La Revue Nègre* opened at the Théâtre des Champs-Élysées starring twenty-five young artists. Among them were the jazz musicians Sidney Bechet and Claude Hopkins and a young African-American dancer from St. Louis named Josephine Baker.

Before the night was over, Baker had stunned Paris. In the *Dance Sauvage*, she writhed about a half-naked man; at another point she danced with a pink flamingo feather clenched between her thighs. Paris had never seen anything like her.

In the crowd was twenty-two-year-old Georges Simenon, who—like most everyone in the audience—was captivated. He immediately headed backstage, where he wasted little time in courting her. Although the twenty-year-old Baker would overnight become the star of Parisian nightlife, she was drawn to the lesser-known Simenon.

"Hers is, without question, the world's most famous butt, and the most desired," Simenon bragged to a fan magazine. He wrote:

> Josephine Baker is a burst of laughter, from her comically lacquered hair to her nervous legs, whose curves we cannot see because they are never still. She is a wild child hurtling through the world, carried from continent to continent to continent, dropping into a solemn salon, being hoisted in an egg to the ceiling of a music hall. And we all rush to see her, eyes gleaming in the very same way. Palms sweaty with the same desire. A thousand pairs of opera glasses and naked eyes focus on her, and trembling fingers reach out to her.

The couple planned to launch a magazine, *Le Joséphine Baker's Magazine*. Simenon would be the sole journalist, working out of the magazine "headquarters" at the place des Vosges apartment he shared with his wife, Tigy. But when the magazine launch fell through, Simenon reexamined his relationship with Baker, whose star far eclipsed his own: "I had become the friend of Josephine Baker, whom I would have married but for my refusal, unknown as I was, to become Mr. Baker."

The affair ended after a year.

Site of the Anthropometric Ball

33, rue Vavin (6th arr.)
Métro: Vavin or Notre-Dame-des-Champs

Although Simenon's prolific sexual appetite eventually earned him nearly as much fame as his books (he is said to be the man of 400 books and 10,000 women), it was his extraordinary productivity and unconventional salesmanship that won him attention early in his career. Among the more

Tigy: *Georges Simenon*.
Reproduced with permission of John Simenon.

notorious of these stunts occurred in 1927, when a Parisian newspaper announced that Simenon would complete a novel while living in a glass cage for three days and three nights—a feat he never actually undertook.

He thought of a more successful promotion in February 1931: the Anthropometric Ball. It was advertised as the greatest "prison gathering ever," and Simenon stopped at nothing to make the event convincing. Invitations resembling summonses and police booking cards instructed the 1,000 guests to head to La Boule Blanche, a West Indian nightclub in the up-and-coming neighborhood of Montparnasse.

The walls of La Boule Blanche were covered with pictures of handcuffs, bloody handprints, and headless corpses. A fake pimp, prostitute, and bloody butcher were installed at the door, as were fake policemen who demanded guests' fingerprints. The party grew wild as the night wore on: Le Dôme waiters rushed about replenishing the buffet; guests threw off their clothes and danced in showers of champagne; and Simenon's fauvist friend Derain began a portrait on one woman's bathing suit.

Throughout it all, Simenon sat calmly on the mezzanine, pipe in his mouth, smoking and signing copies of his books.

The wild nights of La Boule Blanche ended years ago, and today the site is home to a baby clothes store.

Gallimard

5, rue Sébastien-Bottin (7th arr.)
T: 01 49 54 42 00
Métro: Rue du Bac

Georges Simenon walked into the offices of France's most prestigious publisher, Gallimard, in 1933 ready to make a deal with its boss. Gaston Gallimard greeted Simenon and suggested they head to lunch, assuming the contract could be worked out over a fine meal and sufficient flattery of his prospective author. Simenon stopped him short:

> To begin with, we will never share a meal. I detest business lunches where everything but business is discussed, to be followed by an appointment for another business lunch. The contract will be discussed in your office, in the presence of a secretary, with the door closed and the phone off the hook. . . . In addition, I will never call you Gaston, as everyone here seems to do, nor will I ever say "my good friend" to you, since I also detest that kind of talk.

Le Grand Véfour

17, rue de Beaujolais (1st arr.)
T: 01 42 96 56 27
Métro: Pyramides or Palais-Royal

It was the first Tuesday of the month, and as usual, René Maugras was dining at Le Grand Véfour. It was a prestigious location befitting the powerful newspaper publisher and his friends, all members of Paris's elite. The decor dated to the eighteenth century, and its windows looked out onto the Palais-Royal. The fifty-five-year-old man excused himself but did not return. He was later found lying unconscious on the bathroom floor.

Although Simenon is best remembered as a detective fiction writer, he wrote several literary novels as well. Considered to be one of the finest examples of his work, *The Bells of Bicêtre* (1963) tells of a powerful newspaper publisher who becomes an invalid.

The novel was partly based on a true story. In order to make the novel

as convincing as possible, Simenon—
who was no longer living in Paris—
made a day-trip to the Bicêtre hospital
and studied everything from the routine of the hospital workers to the
sound of the tolling church bells. He
pored over medical textbooks in order
to provide lengthy descriptions of the
publisher's condition.

He also contacted the head chef
of Le Grand Véfour, a favorite of
Napoleon, Colette, Jean Cocteau, and
Victor Hugo. Chef Raymond Oliver—
who is still spoken of in reverential
tones by Parisians—provided him with
menus of the Tuesday gatherings,
which Simenon dutifully recorded in
his novel. Today, only one of Oliver's
original dishes—the pigeon Prince
Rainier III—remains on the menu.

Traces of the restaurant's literary
clientele can be found throughout the
restaurant, from the red velvet ban-
quettes bearing the names of Victor
Hugo and Colette to the white ceramic
ashtrays representing George Sand's
hands and designed by Jean Cocteau.

At the launch party held for the
book at the chic Hotel George V (31,
avenue George V), Simenon recalled
his novel's theme in his greeting to
journalists:

I'm glad you're on time. I don't mind
having my wallet or some other object
of value stolen, but not my time.
Objects can be replaced, but who
knows how much time any of us
has left?

Simone de Beauvoir
(1908–1986)

Jean-Paul Sartre
(1905–1980)

Paris was liberated now; the world and the future had been handed back to us, and we flung ourselves upon them.

—Simone de Beauvoir
The Prime of Life, 1960

The jury that assembled in 1929 to judge philosophy candidates for the *agrégation* (France's selective examination for secondary education positions) was split over to who should be awarded first place. Clever twenty-one-year-old Simone de Beauvoir, the youngest in her class, was known as Castor (the beaver), for her industriousness. Jean-Paul Sartre, two years her elder, impressed the jury with his extraordinary intelligence but presented them with less rigorous arguments. In the end, the jury chose Sartre. But as one member later said, "Everybody agreed that, of the two, she was the real philosopher."

Sartre and Beauvoir began to study together while students at the École Normale Supérieure and the Sorbonne, respectively. Beauvoir was known around campus as a badly dressed, blue-eyed beauty; Sartre was just shy of five feet tall, with a pockmarked complexion and teeth stained by years of chain-smoking. Even then, his reputation with women was legendary—he would, Beauvoir later remarked, seduce women by explaining their souls to them.

Sartre and Beauvoir fell in love shortly after the *agrégation* exam. They both took teaching jobs and for a few years split their time between Paris and various provincial towns. Even when living in the same city, they agreed to keep separate apartments: "So we had all the advantages of sharing our lives, but none of the inconveniences," Beauvoir later recalled in *The Prime of Life*. In fact, throughout their fifty-year relationship, each would take other lovers, then meet with each other to share details and analyze the new partners.

A decade after their triumph in the *agrégation* exam, both Beauvoir and Sartre were living in Paris, working on novels in the back booths of Le Dôme or La Rotonde. This routine was briefly disrupted when Sartre was called up for duty in 1939. He returned in 1941, however, and together the two resumed their daily café-writing—albeit in a Paris occupied by the Nazis and suffering from food, fuel, transportation, and electricity shortages. He and Beauvoir soon abandoned Le Dôme for the Café Flore, as Le Dôme was overrun, Sartre wrote, with Germans who "were tactless enough to bring their own tea and coffee, and to have these prepared and served in front of us Frenchmen, who were already reduced to drinking some anonymous and ghastly substitute."

Under the Occupation, stores and bars were closed. Beauvoir became an inventive cook, making do with what food she could find, while Sartre searched in the gutters and under seats for cigarette butts so that he could smoke his pipe. "There was no one in Paris without a relation or a friend who had been arrested or deported or shot," wrote Sartre.

Sartre attempted to begin a resistance movement, *Socialisme et Liberté*—jokingly known by its handful of followers as the "Central Committee of the Sartre Group"—whose most ambitious effort included a one-hundred-page draft for a new French constitution. A more serious effort was their contributions to *Combat*, the newspaper of the underground Resistance movement, which their friend Albert Camus was affiliated with. On August 18, 1944, Sartre wrote, "I describe only what I've seen. It begins like a holiday, and, today still, the Boulevard St.-Germain, deserted and intermittently swept by machine-gun fire, keeps an appearance of tragic solemnity."

Both writers mined the experience of the Occupation in their writing:

Beauvoir in *The Blood of Others* (1945), about two lovers caught up in the Paris Resistance, and Sartre in *The Flies* (1943). Sartre and Beauvoir argued in their Occupation works that man defines himself and the world through his individual actions. The philosophy, which Sartre had developed during the war, held that in a world without gods or the possibility of transcendence, man is absolutely free but must accept responsibility for his choices. In the aftermath of World War II, this thinking was quickly embraced by a young generation of French.

But while existentialism dominated French intellectual discourse over the coming decade, it would become a fashionable youth movement, associated with left-leaning non-conformists. In the *caves* of St.-Germain, artists, writers, and students listened to jazz (which had been banned by the Nazis), danced the jitterbug, and developed a wardrobe consisting of black turtlenecks, berets, jeans for the men and flowing skirts for the women.

The proof of existentialism's vogue came on May 3, 1947, when the Paris paper *Samedi-Soir* published the "existentialists' time-table," detailing

their movements: Café Flore from 11am to 1pm, lunch at Les Assassins, late evening at the Bar Vert or the Tabou (a new club opened by Sartre's friend the writer and musician Boris Vian). The piece was accompanied by a photo of singer Juliette Greco and actor Roger Vadim, "exchanging depressing thoughts" at the entrance of one of the cellar clubs of St.-Germain, where "the existentialists, doubtless waiting for the atomic bomb which is dear to them, now drink, dance, love, and sleep."

Beauvoir and Sartre spent little time in the typical existentialist cafés and *caves*, which were increasingly frequented by young American students toting copies of Sartre's *Being and Nothingness* (1942). Sartre's extraordinarily influential work overshadowed that of Beauvoir, despite the success of her postwar novels. In St.-Germain, she was primarily known as "Sartre's woman"—or, by those who believed she controlled the writer, as "Notre Dame de Sartre" and "La Grande Sartreuse."

Simone de Beauvoir, August 1947.

However, *The Second Sex* (1949), which described the history of female oppression, brought Beauvoir greater recognition—and a hailstorm of criticism in a France not yet ready for women's liberation. The second volume, which began with the statement "You are not born, but become a woman," asserted that femininity is not a genetic but a social construction, and that idea became a rallying cry for the feminist movement.

In the meantime, Sartre had begun to turn away from novel- and play-writing, having decided that literature was a bourgeois convention. Instead, he devoted his time to unconventional biographies and *Les Temps modernes*, the review he had begun in 1944 to promote radical thought. *Les Temps modernes* was one of the many forums in which he expressed opposition to the French occupation of Algeria and support of Algerian rebels. Forced into hiding, he and Beauvoir moved from one Parisian apartment to the next. Throughout the 1960s they traveled the world in support of revolution and leftist causes and Sartre made headlines by refusing the Nobel Prize in 1964. Just four years later, he would be cited as a key influence in the May 1968 rebellion in France.

In their later years, Sartre and Beauvoir spent less time together, although they still met on Saturday evenings at Beauvoir's apartment on the rue Schoelcher to listen to music, and at La Coupole on Sundays.

In 1965, Sartre adopted his young lover, Arlette Elkaïm, a move that effectively turned over posthumous control of his writings and papers to his new daughter—and not to the woman with whom he had already spent nearly forty years of his life, and who had been his tireless supporter and editor.

Nevertheless, Beauvoir ultimately defended Sartre, and even served as a sponsor for the adoption. Sartre died in 1980; Beauvoir died nearly six years to the day after him. The two share a tombstone in the Montparnasse cemetery.

Sites

Café Flore

172, boulevard St.-Germain (6th arr.)
T: 01 45 48 55 26
Métro: St.-Germain-des-Prés

When Sartre was called up for military duty during the war, Beauvoir spent many of her days reading philosophy books at the shabby but heated Le Dôme or at the Bibliothèque Nationale. One afternoon while walking back to her hotel room, she decided to stop for a coffee at Café Flore.

Entering the café, she was immediately taken by how warm it was. Although it was filled with German soldiers, she decided to make it her new place to write and arrived each morning at 8am so that she could claim one of the two tables near the stove. When Sartre returned in 1941, he joined her there, and as regulars the two were allowed to hide in the upstairs salon while all other customers were forced to take shelter in the St.-Germain métro station.

"It's a milieu of indifference, where other people exist without troubling me while I don't worry about them," said

Sartre. "Anonymous drinkers who argue noisily at the next table disturb me less than a wife and children who would walk about on tiptoe so as not to disturb me."

After the publication of *She Came to Stay* in 1943, Beauvoir became so well known that people began to make specific trips to Café Flore to see her. While at first she was surprised by all the attention, she quickly grew weary of the interruptions and would give visitors a fifteen- or twenty-minute appointment for later that day or another day.

Hôtel du Pont-Royal

7, rue de Montalembert (7th arr.)
T: 01 42 84 70 00
www.hotel-pont-royal.com
Métro: Rue du Bac

When constant interruptions from fans and curious onlookers made work at Café Flore difficult, Beauvoir and Sartre switched to the bar of the Hôtel du Pont-Royal. The tables were little more than wooden kegs, but the bar offered a quiet that the Flore and Deux Magots had lost around the time the American tour buses began to circle St.-Germain.

One day, the American author Truman Capote wandered in and spot-ted the famous couple. He disliked them almost instantly:

> At the time the Pont-Royal had a leathery little basement bar that was the favored swill bucket of haute Bohème's fatbacks. Walleyed, pipe-sucking, pasty-hued Sartre and his spinsterish moll, de Beauvoir, were usually propped in a corner like an abandoned pair of ventriloquist's dolls.

Nor was the couple impressed by Capote. Beauvoir was fascinated by his mannerisms and clothes, and said he looked like a "white mushroom" in his bulky white sweater and powder-blue velvet pants. Sartre, Capote later gossiped, had called him a "fairy Existentialist." (Beauvoir later denied this rumor, crying out, "He did not! He just called him a fairy!")

Théâtre du Vieux-Colombier

21, rue du Vieux-Colombier (6th arr.)
T: 01 44 39 87 00
www.comedie-francaise.fr
Métro: St.-Sulpice

One of the first meetings between Sartre, Beauvoir, and Camus occurred at the Café Flore during the Occupation. Sartre had written a play, *No Exit*, and wanted Camus not only to direct it but also to play the sole male role. Camus accepted, and soon he was rehearsing with Sartre's small cast in Beauvoir's room at Hôtel La Louisiane (which still stands at 60, rue de Seine). However, the project fell apart when one of the cast members was arrested under suspicion of collaborating with the Resistance. By the time the cast member was released, a new cast had been assembled and Camus had backed out, claiming he was not professional enough to direct at the Théâtre du Vieux-Colombier, an avant-garde theater that had since taken up Sartre's play.

In May 1944, *No Exit* made its premiere. Although the work was based on Sartre's existential philosophy, it was also influenced by his own experience of occupied Paris and the oppressive mood of surveillance that hung over the city. The setting is a drawing room decorated in Second Empire style, but the location is hell. The three characters—two women and one man—cannot escape each other, leading one to declare "Hell is—other people!" The play was received enthusiastically by Parisians, who found it amusing that in a city struck by shortages, in Sartre's hell, the lights managed to stay on all the time.

Today, the Vieux-Colombier is one of the three performance halls of the Comédie-Française. The short street is hidden away from the traditional theater spots along the Grands Boulevards.

Sorbonne
1, rue Victor Cousin (5th arr.)
www.paris4.sorbonne.fr/en
Métro: Cluny-la-Sorbonne

Students had long complained about overcrowding, lack of facilities, and the difficult admissions process for Parisian universities. In 1968 when a demonstration at the University of Paris at Nanterre turned violent, students at the centuries-old Sorbonne took up the cause and began demonstrations of their own. On May 6, riots raged throughout the day. Students railed against the administration's lack of responsiveness, identifying their struggle with the war in Vietnam and espousing a variety of leftist thought ranging from anarchism to communism. Sartre took to the airwaves on May 12 to urge students to destroy the university system.

The students occupied the Sorbonne and flew red flags over the chapel and the statues. During the first few days a festive atmosphere reigned as jazz and dance music were played, and sympathetic Parisians brought meals and drinks to the students. Students camped out at the university, setting up press offices in the lecture rooms. On May 15 they swarmed the place de l'Odéon and occupied the theater, flying a black flag from its roof.

Police brutality toward the students turned many against de Gaulle's regime. Soon the student rebellion spread throughout France. Two-thirds of French workers went on strike, paralyzing the country: garbage cans overflowed and public transport stopped running. With protests and strikes raging throughout the country, France seemed to be heading toward another revolution.

But as de Gaulle's government approached collapse, so did the rebellion—its communal spirit having disintegrated under a lack of a common vision. Beauvoir visited her alma mater on June 10 and said the party had become little more than an "epidemic of lice," filled with "beatniks, whores, tramps . . . drug-traffickers and even abortion."

When elections were held at the end of that month, the Gaullist party emerged even stronger than before. Nevertheless, the May of '68 rebellion prompted a major overhaul of the French university system in 1971.

Raymond Depardon: *Fourteenth arrondissement, the funeral of Sartre*, April 19, 1980.
© Raymond Depardon/Magnum Photos.

Richard Wright

(1908–1960)

To live in Paris is to allow one's sensibilities to be nourished by physical beauty. . . . I love my adopted city. Its sunsets, its teeming boulevards, its slow and humane tempo of life have entered deeply into my heart.

—Richard Wright
"I Choose Exile," 1951

Gertrude Stein had long encouraged Richard Wright—the African-American author of *Native Son* (1940) and *Black Boy* (1945)—to come to Paris, and it was she who met the Wright family at the St.-Lazare train station when they arrived in May 1946. Stein took the family to the Trianon Palace Hotel (still at 3, rue de Vaugirard) in St.-Germain, within walking distance from her home. After checking in, Wright went out to explore his new neighborhood, which was filled "with tiny book stores, publishing houses, painters' studios and art shops."

Wright was struck by the sharp contrast between New York City and Paris, which was still reeling from the effects of World War II. His hotel was shabby, with paper-thin walls and a hole in the floor that served as a toilet. Artists crowded the cafés because they did not have heating in their own apartments. And then there were the small peculiarities of life in a foreign country:

The knobs were in the center of the doors! Waiters ladled you your change out of bulging, sagging pockets. Sandwiches were a rough slab of meat flanked by two oblong chunks of bread. Hot milk was used in coffee instead of cream.

As promising as Paris seemed, it was dirty and unstable in the postwar years—not the ideal spot to raise the couple's young daughter. The Wrights returned to New York just six months after arriving in Paris, but found that the US was still an unwelcoming place for an interracial couple. They were back in Paris in July 1947, this time for good.

Paris in 1947 was little improved from what the Wrights had encountered the previous year. There were electricity, gas, and water shortages, and during general strikes garbage piled up on the streets. The family looked for an apartment on the Left Bank while staying with a bookshop owner on 9, rue de Lille. For the equivalent of fifty cents a day, Wright was able to rent a room across the street in which to write. He furnished the room with a typewriter, a bookcase, and reams of paper, as well as a phonograph player for his French-language records and a telescope for spying on his neighbors. But he abandoned his writing studio—and their home across the street—when he discovered that the landlady was receiving visits from a "doctor" who gave her daily dope injections.

After a brief stay in Neuilly, the Wrights moved in May 1948 to the fourth floor of 14, rue Monsieur-le-Prince in the Latin Quarter (today a plaque on the building honors Wright). Rue Monsieur-le-Prince was a narrow street between the Luxembourg Gardens and the Odéon, and Wright's front windows looked out onto the stone walls of the Sorbonne's École de Médecine. Soon Wright had picked *his* café—a decision of utmost importance, as he explained:

At the outset of his sojourn in Paris a foreigner does not at once select his favorite café. The determination of a café in which to spend one's hours of relaxation is a delicate problem, a matter of trial and error, tasting, testing the nature and quality of the café's atmosphere.

He was already well acquainted with the cafés Flore and Deux Magots (or "Deux Maggots," as he spelled it), but those touristy spots were too noisy for his taste. He settled on the Monaco, which was located at the end of his street, close to the intersection with the boulevard St.-Germain. It was a run-of-the-mill café, frequented by working-class Parisians and the many expatriates then milling about the quarter.

Soon Wright was holding court at the Monaco, carelessly waving his cigarette as he argued loudly about politics or women. "Dick greeted everyone with boisterous condescension; it was obvious he was the king thereabouts," said the black detective novelist Chester Himes. Wright brought both Himes and the cartoonist Ollie Harrington to the Café Monaco, and the café soon became a major center for African-Americans to meet in the Latin Quarter.

Wright was welcomed by France's intellectuals. He helped to establish *Présence Africaine*, a journal intended to raise French consciousness about Africa, and took his existentialist philosopher friends Jean-Paul Sartre and Simone de Beauvoir to Chez Honey, an art gallery and nightclub on the rue Jules-Chaplain, where the likes of Kenny Clarke, Duke Ellington, and Lena Horne played to a racially mixed crowd.

But the clubs, cafés, projects— and women—occupying Wright's time were distractions, and more than five years passed before he turned out a new novel. Then in 1953, *The Outsiders* appeared in bookstores. Although the book was set in New York, it had been written in Paris. Critics claimed that Wright was out of touch with America and that the book's bleak vision owed more to French existentialism than to the current racial situation in New York.

A similar criticism would be leveled at *The Long Dream* (1958), which some claimed was an outdated picture of racism in the South. But Wright couldn't win: when he proposed writing a dramatically different novel, told from the perspective of the Aztec king Montezuma, his publisher gently suggested he look toward the subjects of his earlier works.

Wright felt Paris had given him a new perspective on race relations in the US. In a 1951 essay, "I Choose Exile," published in *Ebony*, he wrote: "I tell you frankly that there is more freedom in one square block of Paris than there is in the entire United States of America."

In the fall of 1959 Wright left his large home on the rue Monsieur-le-Prince and moved to a one-bedroom apartment on the small and quiet rue Régis, near St.-Placide. His Underwood typewriter and paintings were still on view, but the apartment at 4, rue Régis was a far more modest dwelling, and one which would not financially drain Wright, who had grown apart from his wife but was supporting her and their daughters, who were living in London. The area then, as now, was filled with galleries and specialty shops, and still allowed Wright walks in the Luxembourg Gardens.

In those days, Wright could be spotted at the Café Tournon, which had replaced the Monaco as his favorite café. Although no longer in existence, the café was located at the top of the rue Tournon, just downstairs from a hotel of the same name. Its tacky, colorful decor was hard to miss. Bad paintings of the Luxembourg Gardens hung on the walls, while a pinball machine dinged and banged throughout the day. Wright tended to stop by in the afternoon, where he would often see his cartoonist friend, Ollie Harrington, sitting in the corner, pipe in one hand, a coffee or dry martini in the other. He told his Café Tournon friends that the Latin Quarter was full of CIA informers posing as regular café-goers.

Although Wright's friends laughed at his "paranoid" rants, there was some truth behind his claims. Wright had been connected to the Communist Party years earlier in Chicago but later severed ties and became an outspoken anti-Communist. Nevertheless, his frequent comments about the racial situation in the US made him a target during the McCarthy era, and while in Paris he received a visit from David Schine, who was working with Roy Cohn in rounding up Communists for Joseph McCarthy and the House Un-American Activities Committee. It is also now believed that Wright's Paris apartment was at one point bugged.

By the late 1950s, Wright wanted to leave Paris. His reasons were many. The city was too distracting for his work, spies were following his every move, and the city—tense during the French-Algerian war—no longer felt welcoming.

The loneliness Wright felt during his last years was captured in his still unpublished work, *Island of Hallucination*, which he began in the late 1950s. It was a semi-autobiographical novel about an African-American born in the South and now living in France. It was also Wright's one truly Parisian novel,

set within Paris and incorporating various experiences and acquaintances drawn from Wright's time there.

In Paris he went in and out of bars, offices, cafés, hotels, and restaurants free of that dogging racial constraint that had been his all his life.

Yet he was not at ease. Beneath his daily bantering there ebbed a secret tide of melancholy that he could not stay. He had not an iota of homesickness, but, deep down, he had to admit that he was not truly in or of France; he knew that he could never be French even if he lived in France a million years. He loved France and the French, yet France was always psychologically distant in his mind.

Sites

Chez Haynes

3, rue Clauzel (9th arr.)
T: 01 48 78 40 63
Métro: St.-Georges

Montmartre, where Josephine Baker first got her start and Bricktop opened a jazz club, had been the heart of the African-American expatriate scene in Paris in the 1920s and 1930s. Soon, it also became the home of France's first soul food restaurant. Opened by an ex-football star, Leroy Haynes, in 1949, Chez Haynes (or "Soulsville in Paris," as some called it) drew black and white Americans, as well as curious French looking to discover chitterlings, corn bread, and collard greens.

Richard Wright was a frequent guest at the restaurant, having befriended Leroy Haynes shortly after the latter's arrival in Paris. He frequently made the trek up the Montparnasse hill to share Georgia catfish or barbecued pig's feet and talk about the two men's common interests —women and sex. Chez Haynes is also where jazz musician Bill Coleman celebrated his marriage in 1953, Louis Armstrong sometimes stopped by for a chat, and Brigitte Bardot tried her first serving of chitterlings and lemon meringue pie.

In 1964, Chez Haynes moved from the rue Manuel to its current address at 3, rue Clauzel in the 9th arrondissement. On the walls hang vintage photos of America's legendary black jazzmen, many of whom came to Paris, like Wright, to escape racism and social constraints.

Wright's former residence

4, rue Régis (6th arr.)
Métro: St.-Placide

It was late November of 1960 when an unexpected visitor rang the door at Wright's apartment. It was the poet Langston Hughes, who took one look at Wright, who was dressed in a suit and lying on his bed, and cried, "Man! You look like you are ready to go to glory!"

Hughes's words later seemed prophetic. Wright left a few minutes afterward for a shabby and obscure Parisian clinic, where he died a few days later.

The Eugène Gibez clinic had been chosen by a shadowy Russian doctor who had few other patients than Wright, whom he had been treating for an amoebic dysentery Wright had acquired on a recent trip to Africa. Wright was to spend the weekend in the clinic, and had told Julia he would call Monday evening. But no call came and later that evening, his doctor declared him dead from a heart attack.

Rumors flew that Wright's death was intentional, carried out by the CIA or FBI, who had been watching Wright's movements since the writer's days in New York. The clinic nurse reported that a mysterious Hungarian woman had visited him earlier that evening— some immediately suspected that the woman may have injected Wright with a heart attack–inducing drug. (According to Wright's money-changer friend, it was a prostitute who was delivering Wright $500 that had been changed into francs.)

Wright's friend Ollie Harrington was among those who suspected foul play. On Tuesday morning Harrington had received a telegram from Wright— "Ollie please come to see me as soon as you get this." Wright had asked him on several occasions to make sure his vomit and urine were analyzed if anything happened to him. But his wife had not requested an autopsy, a decision she was later said to regret.

Richard Wright is buried in the southeast corner of Père-Lachaise.

Albert Camus

(1913–1960)

To know how to remain alone for a year in a poor room teaches a man more than a hundred literary salons and forty years of experience of "Parisian life."

—Albert Camus, 1940

"Black trees in the gray sky and the pigeons colored like the sky. Statues in the grass and that melancholic elegance." Albert Camus' early impressions of Paris evoked the loneliness of a young man isolated from his family and country.

Born in Algeria to parents of Spanish and French origin, Camus was a *pied noir*—a French citizen born in one of France's African colonies. He came to Paris as a journalist in 1940 to join the staff of the *Paris-Soir* newspaper, many of whom had been called up to fight in World War II. He did not stay long, returning in early 1941 to Algeria, where he continued work on a novel, *The Stranger* (1942), that had kept him busy during his lonely days in Paris.

When Camus returned to Paris two years later it was as a minor celebrity. *The Stranger*, about "the nakedness of man faced with the absurd," had been published to great success the previous year, as had *The Myth of Sisyphus* (1942). His message—that humans search in vain to find reason in existence—resonated with occupied Paris, where daily life was now dominated by concerns over food and fuel shortages. He received a similar reaction from the French public with his post-war novel, *The Plague* (1947). Although the novel contained no direct references to occupied Paris, readers had little trouble interpreting the allegory about a city struck by plague:

> *The silent city was no more than an assemblage of huge, inert cubes, between which only the mute effigies of great men, carapaced in bronze, with their blank stone or metal faces, conjured up a sorry semblance of what the man had been. In lifeless squares and avenues these tawdry idols lorded it under the lowering sky; stolid monsters that might have personified the rule of immobility imposed on us, or, anyhow, its final aspect, that of a defunct city in which plague, stone, and darkness had effectively silenced every voice.*

Camus' success in the mid-1940s came as a shock to the French literary world—and not only because of his *pied noir* accent, colorful Algerian suits, and occasional black eye from a bar fight. Whereas much of French literature was then dominated by well-educated bourgeois, Camus rose to prominence from a working-class background. Such a rise would have been improbable in class-conscious Paris, but in young, colonial Algeria he had been able to acquire the newspaper and theater jobs that in Paris were typically only open to the bourgeoisie.

During the final stretch of the war, Camus' days were occupied by a job with the publisher Gallimard, while his nights were spent working on *The Plague* and *Combat*, the underground newspaper of the Resistance. What little free time he had was spent at the Café Flore or other St.-Germain spots with his new writer friends, the existentialists Jean-Paul Sartre and Simone de Beauvoir, with whom he would later break.

"What the heart requires, at certain times, are places without poetry," Camus had told the *New Yorker* in 1946, and by the 1950s he had grown very weary of Paris and the demands it placed on his time. He was continually asked to intervene on behalf of various social causes, in particular the resistance movement gaining force in Algeria. A French colony since the mid-nineteenth century, the country was one of the last to gain independence. For years following World War II, the French government had been promising to make important reforms in the country and to grant its native population more rights. But when little came of the promises, the National Liberation Front (FLN) struck at colonial French establishments, provoking retaliation from the *pied noir* community.

While Camus was outspoken regarding Fascist Spain, he was largely silent on the Algeria issue, refusing to support either the FLN terrorists or the oppressive colonialist regime—winning him enemies on both sides. Although Camus had been one of the first French writers to push for equal treatment of North African Moslems, as a *pied noir* with family in Algeria, he could not condone violence against the French still living there. "I believe in justice," he said, "but I shall defend my mother above justice."

In 1957 he was awarded the Nobel Prize, but he was writing less and was suffering from attacks of claustrophobia. In the late fall of 1959, he left for Provence, where he hoped he would finally find the peace to work on a new novel. He was returning to Paris on January 4, 1960, when his car crashed, killing him instantly. In his briefcase the police found an early draft of *The First Man*, an unfinished, partly autobiographical novel in which he intended to describe French Algeria to mainland France and show that the French Algerian is a man without a past, fully belonging to neither the colony nor its metropole.

Sites

Hôtel Minerve

13, rue des Écoles (5th arr.)
T: 01 43 26 26 04
www.hotel-paris-minerve.com
Métro: Cardinal-Lemoine

When Camus moved to Paris in the fall of 1943, it was a changed, occupied Paris that he discovered. He soon moved into the Hôtel Minerve on the rue des Écoles, in part for its convenient, ten-minute walk from his new job at Gallimard (he would never live more than a twenty-minute walk away from the publisher's offices). The elderly woman who owned the hotel was sympathetic to the Resistance cause and rented many rooms to activists.

The Occupation was a difficult time for Camus, as it was for most other Parisians. Daily life was filled with shortages and uncertainty. His hotel room had no bath or toilet, let alone heating, and when friends came by to visit the men would often talk with their overcoats pulled up to their ears.

Camus later recalled the Occupation as "neither a good nor a bad time. It was the absence of time. Or a time without color and without date, a time when one wound up the alarm clock every night, but when the calendar was false."

Combat Headquarters

100, rue de Réaumur (2nd arr.)
Métro: Sentier or Réaumur-Sébastopol

The *Combat* newspaper grew out of an underground Resistance movement of the same name, which was created in 1942 to sabotage the German war effort. Published sporadically during the war, it became a daily paper once Paris was liberated, and a generation of young French would rally behind its battle cry "From Resistance to Revolution."

As the Germans began their withdrawal from Paris, the *Combat* staff set up headquarters on the rue de Réaumur in a building formerly occupied by the collaborationist press—and still technically under German control. When the staff entered they discovered cases of grenades in the office, as well as several German uniforms—perhaps left behind by German soldiers who had preferred to flee Paris in civilian clothes.

Rushing to ready the magazine for publication, the staff spent the first few nights sleeping atop old newspapers and living on rations left behind in the cafeteria. On August 21, the first issue was sold by hawkers between the rue de Rivoli and the avenue de l'Opéra. All of the copies disappeared within one hour. The keys to the safe could not be found, and when money started coming in from sales the staff kept it in wastebaskets.

The editorials in the following days were anonymous (all of the initial *Combat* articles would be) but were written by the editor-in-chief, Albert Camus:

> Paris fires all of its bullets in the August night. Against this immense backdrop of stones and fountains, all about this river whose waters are heavy with history, the barricades of freedom, one more time, have been raised. One more time, justice must be purchased with the blood of men.

Camus stayed with the paper until 1947. Today the old *Combat* headquarters are now the offices of Paris's large daily, *France-Soir*.

Studio of André Gide

1, *bis* rue Vaneau (7th arr.)
Métro: St.-François-Xavier or Sèvres-Babylone

Before the end of the war, Camus traded in his rundown hotel room at the Hôtel Minerve for a sixth-floor studio at 1, *bis* rue Vaneau in St.-Germain (again, just a few minutes from the Gallimard office). The high-ceilinged studio was unremarkable save for a trapeze hanging from the middle of the ceiling and the identity of its owner: André Gide, the influential author of *The Pastoral Symphony* and *Fruits of the Earth*.

The studio was connected to the main apartment, which belonged to Gide and his longtime companion, an eighty-six-year-old woman he called "la petite dame." Forty years separated Camus and Gide, and the two never established a great friendship. Camus wrote that Gide detested "that noisy promiscuity which takes the place of friendship in our world." Nevertheless, the two men were amicable: Gide would good-humoredly bring back Camus' cat when it entered his apartment from the roof; other times he would drop by when he heard Camus' wife, Francine, playing the piano. But most of the time the two writers had little contact, and Camus knew of Gide's doings on the other side of the door only by his "rustlings, the little hustle and bustle of meditation or reverie."

By the time Paris was liberated, Camus' studio had become a meeting place for intellectuals like Sartre and Beauvoir, as well as his Algerian friends. Camus eventually had the trapeze removed, however, because he grew "tired of watching intellectuals who visited me hanging from it."

Camus' former residence
18, rue Séguier (6th arr.)
Métro: St.-Michel

In 1946, Albert and Francine Camus moved to 18, rue Séguier, a town house owned by Camus' publisher and friends, the Gallimards. The Camus apartment ran alongside one wing of the house, with windows facing both the courtyard and the street.

The stately building was more beautiful than it was practical. Once a mansion, it had extraordinarily high ceilings and was impossible to heat, making winter a particularly trying time for Camus, who suffered from tuberculosis. In addition, his four years at the rue Séguier apartment coincided with a difficult period professionally. His new fame made him in constant demand in Paris. Now in his mid-thirties, he was writing less and less fiction—his time instead devoted to *Combat*, long nights

in St.-Germain, and various social concerns.

Years later, Sartre evoked the rue Séguier apartment in one of his most autobiographical stories, "The Artist at Work." The story tells of a successful painter, Jonas, who becomes a victim of his success. He is bombarded by lunches and visits and requests to denounce various social injustices. At thirty-five, he lives in a cramped apartment in an eighteenth-century building:

> The rooms, particularly high-ceilinged, and equipped with superb windows, had certainly been designed, if one judged by their majestic proportions, for pomp and ceremony.

As he approached the end of his life, Camus felt increasingly suffocated by Paris and his life there, telling a friend, "For several years now, my work hasn't freed me, it has enslaved me." He grew weary of the crusader reputation he had earned: "I am exasperated by this reputation of austerity and of virtue—of which I am quite unworthy —and that I am constantly being beaten over the head with by well-intentioned people."

Café Flore

172, boulevard St.-Germain (6th arr.)
T: 01 45 48 55 26
Métro: St.-Germain-des-Prés

Camus' association with the philosophers Jean-Paul Sartre and Simone de
Beauvoir would lead many—particularly those abroad—to wrongly associ-
ate him with existentialist philosophy.
While he emphatically denied this connection, his claims were often muted
by his frequent visits to Parisian bars
and clubs known for their existentialist
crowd. Although Sartre had Beauvoir,
and Camus, his wife, Francine, the two
spent many nights together drinking at
the Café Flore and chasing starlets.

"He was simple and merry,"
Beauvoir later recalled. "He called
the waiter named Pascal at the Flore
'Descartes,' but he could afford to do
this; his charm, due to a happy mix of
nonchalance and enthusiasm, guaran-
teed him against vulgarity.

The famous threesome was eventually driven apart by politics. There
was, some said, an element of jealousy on Sartre's part. Camus was the
younger, more handsome of the two,
and had actively participated in the
Resistance, while Sartre and Beauvoir

had watched American movies and
bicycled in the countryside as Hitler
invaded Poland. In 1952, the year
that Sartre openly declared himself a
Communist, Camus published a clearly
anti-Communist text, *The Rebel*. Sartre
openly attacked Camus' position and
accused him of "pomposity, which is
natural to you." Camus retaliated by
calling Sartre one of the critics "who
have never pointed anything but their
armchairs in the direction of history."

All of Paris talked of the break, and
at St.-Germain cafés like the Café Flore
intellectuals took sides.

James Baldwin

(1924–1987)

In some deep, black, stony, and liberating way, my life, in my own eyes, began during that first year in Paris.

—*James Baldwin*
"Equal in Paris," 1955

The twenty-four-year-old meat-packer, elevator boy, book critic, and aspiring writer who landed in Paris on Armistice Day, November 11, 1948, had only $40 in his pocket. James Baldwin spoke no French, but that did not worry him. He felt he had learned all he needed to know about France by reading Honoré de Balzac's *The Human Comedy* and was sure that the country could offer a better life than New York, where he had drifted between the white Greenwich Village literary crowd and the black Harlem community in which he was raised.

Met by a friend at the airport, Baldwin was immediately led to St.-Germain-des-Prés and to Richard Wright, who was holding court that day in Deux Magots. Baldwin and Wright were already acquainted, having met in New York a few years earlier. The successful author of *Native Son* had even read some pages of Baldwin's half-finished book, an early version of *Go Tell It on the Mountain.* Wright, one of the few African-American authors to have been embraced by the mainstream American literary scene, was one of Baldwin's literary heroes.

Wright introduced Baldwin to a friend, Themistocles Hoetis, who helped Baldwin find a hotel close by on the rue du Dragon. Hoetis asked him to contribute to *Zero,* the literary magazine he was founding. Baldwin had only just arrived and already Paris seemed promising.

But three days after his arrival, Baldwin had run through his $40 and did not know where to turn for cash. (This would be a recurring theme throughout his nine years in Paris.) His career as a book critic was not feasible in France, since no publication was willing to send a book across the Atlantic and then sit around waiting for Baldwin's review. Nor could he write for the French journals—in addition to the language barrier, he was not (and, unlike Wright, never would be) in touch with French society or with its intellectuals.

Baldwin decided to put his novel on hold to begin the more lucrative business of essay writing. One of his first pieces proved to be the most controversial. Published in the Spring 1949 inaugural issue of *Zero,* "Everybody's Protest Novel" criticized protest fiction and cited Wright's *Native Son,* whose black hero, said Baldwin, was a caricature.

Wright never fully forgave Baldwin for the essay, and although the two occasionally crossed paths, they were drawn to different social circles in Paris. While Wright befriended French and African intellectuals as well as expatriates, Baldwin lived an expatriate life largely isolated from Parisians. He moved among various groups—black, white, straight, and gay—and enjoyed the comparative absence of racial tension he found in France. "Every Negro in America carries all through his life the burden of race consciousness like a corpse on his back. I shed that corpse when I stepped off the train in Paris," he told the American magazine *Ebony* in 1953. This did not stop him, however, from joking about writing a book entitled *Non, nous ne jouons pas la trompette*—a reference to Parisians' stereotype that all African-Americans abroad were jazz musicians.

But Paris proved to be a distraction, not an inspiration, for his novel, which was about a young man growing up in poverty in Harlem. Baldwin found a quieter setting in Switzerland, where he stayed for a few months and completed *Go Tell It on the Mountain*.

The book was published in 1953 to good reviews, and Baldwin's publishers thought they had discovered the next great African-American author. But Baldwin did not want to be a "black writer" or "political writer," and certainly not the "next Richard Wright." He defiantly set his next book in France, not Harlem or the American South, and made all of his characters white.

Giovanni's Room (1956) was set in Baldwin's expatriate Paris—a cosmopolitan crowd consisting of mainly white Europeans and Americans. His only novel set in Paris, *Giovanni's Room* provides a window onto Baldwin's own distant relationship to the Paris of Parisians. Paris, for Baldwin, was dominated by cafés and expatriates; it was the mythic city he had first learned about from Ernest Hemingway and Henry Miller. In *Giovanni's Room*, it is a placed filled with twilights and tragic love, where one sees "time gone by" and where even the most banal of sights—the polluted Seine, for example—are elevated to poetry:

> *The island of the city widened away from us, bearing the weight of the cathedral; beyond this, dimly,*

> *through speed and mist, one made out the individual roofs of Paris, their myriad, squat chimney stacks very beautiful and varicolored under the pearly sky. Mist clung to the river, softening that army of trees, softening those stones, hiding the city's dreadful corkscrew alleys and dead-end streets, clinging like a curse to the men who slept beneath the bridges.*

Baldwin's romantic portrayals of Paris were a far cry from the turmoil in the city in 1956, as debates raged over the Algerian war. Although Baldwin recognized the similarities between the discrimination against Arabs in France and that against blacks in America, his general disinterest in France and in Paris beyond St.-Germain left him distanced from the conflict and the impassioned debates dominating Paris's streets. The more daily news became dominated by the war, the more Baldwin turned away from France and turned toward to the struggles in America, where southern schools were still dragging their heels in implementing the 1954 Supreme Court decision to desegregate all schools. "I realized," said Baldwin, "what tremendous things were happening and that I had a role to play."

Baldwin said goodbye to Paris in July 1957, at age thirty-two. In America, his writing became increasingly political. Ironically, Paris had been the catalyst for this change. As Baldwin wrote in a 1958 essay on desegregation in North Carolina:

"You can take the child out of the country," my elders were fond of saying, "but you can't take the country out of the child." They were speaking of their own antecedents, I supposed; it didn't, anyway, seem possible that they could be warning me; I took myself out of the country and went to Paris. It was there that I discovered that the old folks knew what they were talking about: I found myself, willy-nilly, alchemized into an American the moment I touched French soil.

Sites

Hôtel de Verneuil

8, rue de Verneuil (7th arr.)
T: 01 42 60 82 14
www.hotelverneuil.com
Métro: Rue du Bac or Musée d'Orsay

> The moment I began living in French hotels I understood the necessity of French cafés.
> —"Equal in Paris," 1955

With its café life and expatriate scene, Baldwin took an immediate liking to St.-Germain, and soon after arriving in Paris he settled at a hotel a few blocks away from the Seine on the rue de Verneuil.

At the time, Paris was still recovering from World War II, subject to food rationing and fuel shortages. The Hôtel de Verneuil was no exception. The rooms of the seventeenth-century building were small and unheated, and guests were forced to share a Turkish toilet. Baldwin wrote:

> Paris hotels had never heard of central heating or hot baths or showers or clean towels and sheets or ham and eggs. Their attitude toward electricity was demonic—once one had seen what they thought of as wiring one

wondered why the city had not, long ago, vanished in flame.

But the hotel was known for its cheap rooms and its large expatriate following, and Baldwin made some of his first friends in Paris there. When he fell ill shortly after his arrival in 1948, the owner's wife, Madame Dumont, took care of him and waived his hotel bills. Baldwin later thanked her by naming a character in his 1958 story "This Morning, This Evening, So Soon" after her.

Today guests at the Hôtel de Verneuil will find it far more comfortable than Baldwin did in 1948. Marble bathtubs off each room and Continental breakfast in the *cave* are standard.

Hôtel Bac St.-Germain

66, rue du Bac (7th arr.)
T: 01 42 22 20 03
www.bacstgermain-hotel.com
Métro: Rue du Bac

Returning from a trip in 1949, Baldwin found that his regular quarters at the Hôtel de Verneuil were occupied and that he would need to find a new place to stay. Just a few streets away was the Hôtel Bac, "one of those enormous dark, cold and hideous establishments in which Paris abounds that seem to breathe forth, in their airless, humid, stone-cold halls, the weak light, scurrying chambermaids, and creaking stairs, an odor of gentility long dead."

His good friend the Norwegian journalist Gidske Anderson said the hotel's rooms were as "large as ballrooms in a castle, where the stairs and floors made creaking noises when you stepped on them, and a mildewy smell pervaded the corridors."

Baldwin and Gidske had been planning a small Christmas dinner, but when Gidske went by the hotel a few days before Christmas, she discovered that Baldwin was nowhere to be found. "*Il est sorti*"—he has gone out—was the terse response she received from the hotel owner. Over the next few days, Gidske received the same answer each time she went by, and the owner "always replied in such a way that he made it seem as if Jimmy had just gone out the door."

In fact, Baldwin was nowhere near the hotel but rather in a prison in the outskirts of Paris. He had been arrested after the police discovered a stolen bed sheet in his room at the Hôtel Bac. Baldwin protested, saying

an American friend had given it to him and he had fit it on his mattress in order to alert his hotel, "the Grand Hôtel du Bac," as to "the unpleasant state of its linen." Noticing their sheet had disappeared, the proprietors of the original hotel contacted the police, and an investigation led to Baldwin's room at the rue du Bac.

The court had a good laugh over Baldwin's story and he was released within a week. The story is recalled in his essay "Equal in Paris" and is alluded to in Richard Wright's work *Island of Hallucination*, in which Baldwin was the inspiration for a homosexual, sheet-stealing character named Mechanical.

Renovated in 1989, the Hôtel Bac is today a three-star hotel.

Hôtel d'Alsace (L'Hôtel)
13 rue des Beaux-Arts (6th arr.)
T: 01 44 41 99 00
www.l-hotel.com
Métro: St-Germain-des-Prés or Mabillon

When his New York publishers asked him to revise his manuscript for his first novel, *Go Tell It on the Mountain*, Baldwin agreed and looked to take the first boat back to America to finish the job. As usual, he was out of cash and had no way to pay his Parisian hotel bill.

Baldwin had previously met the American actor Marlon Brando a few times while in the US. Now that Brando was a star, Baldwin figured that the wealthy actor would be able to solve his money problem. As his friend Themistocles Hoetis explained:

> Jimmy picked me up at the Deux-Magots and took me to the Hôtel des Beaux-Arts, off the rue Dauphine. I didn't really know what was happening, but whatever line Jimmy's giving Brando, I'm just there to agree. So the concierge calls up. Brando comes down to the lobby. Hello. Hi. Then Jimmy starts his hustle. . . . He's helping me make a little magazine. We've got no money. We're trying to publish the good young poets and novelists, et cetera. . . . Money was shuffled. We thank him—and it's out into the road.

Baldwin got his "magazine" money, and seven days later he stepped off the boat in New York City.

The hotel of the Brando hustle has seen many celebrities over the past century, including Jorge Borges, Thomas Wolfe, and Oscar Wilde.

Acknowledgements

The author would like to thank
Luke Miner, Deborah Powell, Nadia
Aguiar, and Angela Hederman.

About the Author

Jessica Powell has worked as a journalist, translator, and editor in Europe
and Japan. She is currently based in
Paris and Japan.